Janet M Schreiber PhD
HC 81 Box 631
Questa NM 87556-9705

D0044932

VOLUME 1

BEYOND THE INNOCENCE OF CHILDHOOD:

Factors Influencing Children and Adolescents' Perceptions and Attitudes Toward Death

David W. Adams, M.S.W., C.S.W.
McMaster University
and
Eleanor J. Deveau, R.N., B.Sc.N.
McMaster University

Death, Value and Meaning Series
Series Editor: John D. Morgan

Baywood Publishing Company, Inc.
AMITYVILLE, NEW YORK

Library of Congress Catalog Number: 95-20408
ISBN: 0-89503-128-0 (Cloth)

Library of Congress Cataloging-in-Publication Data

Adams, David Walter, 1942-
   Factors influencing children and adolescents' perceptions and
attitudes toward death / David W. Adams and Eleanor J. Deveau.
      p. cm. - - (Beyond the innocence of childhood ; v. 1)
   Includes bibliographical references and index.
   ISBN 0-89503-128-0 (cloth)
   1. Children and death.   2. Teenagers and death.   3. Death-
-Psychological aspects. I. Deveau, Eleanor J. II. Title.
III. Series: Adams, David Walter, 1942-. Beyond the innocence of
childhood ; v. 1.
BF723.D3A33 1995 vol. 1
155.9'37'083 s- -dc20
[155.9'37'083]
                                           95-20408
                                               CIP

DEDICATION

To Ellie's brother, **Edward Anthony Gzik,** *who will always be remembered for his encouragement, support, friendship, and profound belief and pride in close family ties.*

Foreword

Combining the ideas of *children* and *death* in one sentence challenges our basic understandings of life, death, and God. Western mythology is that we live in a neat, predictable world in which children live blissful lives in the households of loving parents. When death is seen, it is usually seen on television as something remote and something that happens to others.

In areas such as our own, where life expectancy is long, it is possible for children to have limited personal exposure to the death of a significant other until age twenty or thirty. In many places in the world this "innocence of death" is not the case. Our ancestors viewed death as a neighbor, if not always a welcome one. Attitudes to death are shaped not only by exposure to death but more fundamentally by our views about the world and our place in it. We believe that we can be protected from nature, consequently, we have less respect for the power of nature over life. The resulting death attitude system denies us an ***affective consciousness*** of death—the acceptance of the *real probability* of death, and its *appropriateness*.

Parents die. Teachers die. Grandparents die. Even children die. It is clear that our death attitude system today does not provide children with the tools they need at the time of a death. They need to accept the reality that each time they say "goodbye" to someone, it could very well be the last time. When we educate children about death, we are only teaching them about reality. Death is not a mere possibility, but a certainty for all of us. As contributors to this volume show, adults often assume that the idea of death is harmful to children, or that they are incapable of understanding the limits of life. Neither of these is accurate. We merely allow our own fears and insecurities to prevent children from facing reality as it truly is. A more positive approach is described in the following chapters.

Once a child knows about death, his/her world has been irreparably altered. This knowledge of death is the most difficult lesson one must learn. Yet it is only in the realization of the limits of our resources that we can get the most from their use. It is only in the realization of the limits of life that we appreciate the fullness of life. The Trappist monks have a saying that one does not have his/her feet on the ground until after they have put someone into it. It is wrong to hide this truth from our children. They will learn that truth. It should not be in spite of the adults who care for them.

It is an honor to be invited to write a foreword to this first volume of Professor David Adams and Mrs. Eleanor Deveau's *Beyond the Innocence of Childhood: Factors Influencing Children and Adolescents' Perceptions and Attitudes Toward Death* in which the need for, and aspects of, appropriate education about death and bereavement for children are explored. The editors of this volume and the other authors of the chapters constitute a "who's who" of teachers, researchers, and clinicians who care for children. There could be no single person or group more qualified to bring together a number of experts than Professor Adams and Mrs. Deveau.

I believe that this volume makes an outstanding contribution to the knowledge needed by children and their caregivers for a truly human life, a life in which fullness is possible because the parameters are accepted completely.

John D. Morgan, Ph.D.

ACKNOWLEDGMENTS

We owe a debt of gratitude to the contributing authors for sharing their time, effort, and expertise in producing the chapters which appear in the three volumes of this series.

We are indebted to Dr. J. D. (Jack) Morgan who provided support and encouragement at each phase of the development of this project and to Stuart Cohen, President of Baywood Publishing Company and his staff for making this publication a reality.

A special thank you is extended to Dr. Phyllis Blumberg, Professor, Family Medicine and Director, Geriatric Educational Development Unit, Educational Centre for Aging and Health, Faculty of Health Sciences, McMaster University, for her encouragement, understanding, and patience. Our appreciation is extended to R. E. (Ted) Capstick, Chair, Board of Trustees, Greater Hamilton Employee Assistance Consortium and Vice President, Human Resources, Chedoke-McMaster Hospitals; Dr. Nick Kates, Past Chair, Department of Psychiatry, Faculty of Health Sciences, McMaster University; and Dr. Michael Stevens, Senior Staff Specialist and Head, Oncology Unit, Royal Alexandra Hospital for Children, Camperdown NSW, Australia, for their encouragement and continuing support.

We wish to thank J. Richard Small, M.S.W., C.S.W. for his suggestions and advice; Trudy Leask for typing parts of the manuscripts and helping to communicate with the authors; and Lois Wyndam and her staff at Chedoke-McMaster Hospital Library for their bibliographical assistance.

Finally, we are most grateful to our spouses, J. Paul Deveau and M. Anne Adams, for their **patience**, advice, and assistance. With continual support, understanding, and encouragement from Paul, Anne, and our children we were able to immerse ourselves in the thousands of pages of manuscripts and complete a challenging, interesting and, at times, monumental task!

Table of Contents

Introduction   1

**PART A: CHILDREN AND ADOLESCENTS'
            PERCEPTIONS OF DEATH**   7

CHAPTER 1   9
Can You Answer Children's Questions?
Earl A. Grollman

CHAPTER 2 15
Children and Death: Where Have We Been?
Where Are We Now?
  Charles A. Corr

CHAPTER 3 29
Gender Differences in Children's Understanding of Death
  Judith M. Stillion

CHAPTER 4 45
Using Life Experiences as a Way of Helping Children
Understand Death
  Lynne Ann DeSpelder and Albert Lee Strickland

CHAPTER 5 55
Perceptions of Death Through the Eyes of Children
and Adolescents
  Eleanor J. Deveau

PART B: THE INFLUENCE OF SOCIETY AND CULTURE ON CHILDREN AND ADOLESCENTS' PERCEPTIONS AND ATTITUDES TOWARD LIFE-THREATENING ILLNESS AND DEATH **93**

CHAPTER 6 95
Appetite for Destruction: Children and Violent Death
in Popular Culture
Hannelore Wass

CHAPTER 7 109
American Children and Desert Storm: Impressions of
the Gulf Conflict
Gerry R. Cox, Bernard J. Vanden Berk,
Ronald J. Fundis, and Patrick J. McGinnis

CHAPTER 8 123
AIDS and Our Children
Robert Fulton

CHAPTER 9 131
Glimpses of the Impact of Childhood Cancer on the
Child and Family in East Asia
Ida M. Martinson

CHAPTER 10 145
The Renewal of Ritualization: Funerals of the 1990s
O. Duane Weeks

CHAPTER 11 163
Do Children Belong at Funerals?
Bunty Anderson

About the Editors 179

Contributors 181

Index 183

Introduction

BEYOND THE INNOCENCE OF CHILDHOOD is a collection of forty chapters which are divided into three separate volumes. The overall purpose of this series is to answer the question: How do we as educators, clinicians, and other professionals help children and adolescents deal with threat to their lives, dying, death, and bereavement? Prior to introducing the individual chapters contained in Volume 1 it may be helpful to provide an overview of this series by briefly outlining the focus of each volume.

VOLUME 1

The first volume begins by considering the issue of death as a topic for discussion with children and adolescents. Do they think about death-related issues and how do they acquire a mature understanding of death? Various authors present different perspectives on factors such as gender differences, cognitive development, life experiences, and the effect of parents and other adults' attitudes and beliefs toward death.

This volume then moves on to examine influences in today's society that potentially impact on children and adolescents' perceptions and attitudes concerning death. What roles do the media and political conflict play in attitudes toward violence and death? Do young people throw "caution to the wind" in spite of the epidemic of AIDS? How does a culture influence the management of childhood cancer? In closing this volume, the role of traditional death rituals are discussed. Do children and adolescents' participation in these rituals help to facilitate their understanding of, and adjustment to, death?

VOLUME 2

We begin the second volume by discussing the use of therapeutic techniques such as art, story, music, and play in helping children and adolescents cope with life-threatening illness and then consider the cathartic benefits of humor and laughter and the role of pets as a source of empowerment. Camps, as a special place of fun, friendship, support, and hope for children and teens with cancer or HIV/AIDS, provide another therapeutic option. Our attention then shifts to the interventions required to help adolescents whose suicide attempts threaten their own lives and create ripple effects that bring confusion, hurt, and anger into the lives of the people around them. The final chapter in the first part of Volume 2 examines the pain and suffering of seriously ill children and teens. Such experiences move children to another level—a level beyond the innocence of childhood and plunges them into life filled with uncertainty and lack of control.

The second half of this volume addresses the world of dying children and families whose lives are permanently changed and filled with difficult emotions and formidable challenges. Factors are discussed and guidelines are provided for palliative care in the home and hospital. We enter the world of dying teens to try to understand their need to fulfil hopes and dreams and complete developmental tasks in the time remaining. A discussion of the synergistic value of therapeutic imagery emphasizes its value as a source of energy for dying children and adolescents. The question: "Should children and adolescents be told that they are dying?" sets the stage for an in-depth exploration of truthtelling. Following this discussion, caregivers are challenged to incorporate spirituality as an integral component in the care of dying children and their families. Our focus then turns to a description of the development of a free-standing pediatric hospice in North America. This volume closes with an annotated resource of storytelling and reading materials for seriously ill children, adults, and professionals.

VOLUME 3

The final volume focuses on many of the issues that affect children and adolescents who must contend with the death of someone close. These young people face intense feelings and will need to adapt to many changes. Their grief is an ongoing process which is gradually integrated and becomes a part of their lives. The grief of childhood goes on for a long time and may, in fact, be timeless. This volume begins by addressing the phenomenon of anticipatory grief, considers what is required to respect bereaved children and adolescents, and reflects upon the role of religion and spirituality during bereavement. The long-term implications of the death of a brother, sister, or parent are discussed, followed by sensitive accounts of the traumatic impact of the death of a family member from AIDS and suicide. Losses accumulated as a result of domestic violence render an additional dimension to the grief experienced by some children and adolescents. Our attention then turns to the critical role that the school plays in helping students deal with the death of a friend or classmate. This volume closes with a final section on the structure and benefits of support groups for bereaved children and adolescents.

VOLUME 1–PART A:
Children and Adolescents' Perceptions of Death

Childhood is a time of growth, discovery, play, learning, and fun— a time when children explore the world around them through spontaneous and later structured learning, acquire knowledge, learn to understand themselves, establish their role in the family, develop peer and adult relationships, and find their place in the world.

Most of all, childhood is a time when children should be able to be children—free of the worries, concerns, and responsibilities that are part of the adult world. Many parents work very hard to protect their children from the harsh realities of life. Not only do they strive to maintain the innocence of childhood for their children, but perhaps they also strive to maintain it for themselves. To see the world through the eyes of their children is to see the world differently—to appreciate its wonder, excitement, and possibilities.

Since death is not meant to be part of the repertoire of childhood, many parents and adults avoid death-related discussions and inhibit children's involvement. Unfortunately, such avoidance may negatively influence children's long-term understanding and adjustment. On the other hand, adults who are open and honest concerning such issues positively influence children's perceptions, understanding, and attitudes toward death.

Earl Grollman begins volume one by asking a critical question: Can you answer children's questions concerning death? He acknowledges that talking about death may be a complex and disturbing task for many parents and adults but stresses that children and adolescents need our honesty and openness.

Charles Corr considers the transitions in society over time and how these have influenced children and adolescents' perceptions of death. He emphasizes the need to assist children in integrating death-related encounters in productive ways and offers guidelines for future directions.

Judith Stillion provides findings to support the fact that there are gender differences in respect to children's perceptions of death. She raises concerns regarding the socialization of boys and how it impacts on their level of aggression and their death-related attitudes and experiences.

Life can provide a natural training ground for young children to question issues related to death. Lynne DeSpelder and Albert Strickland address children's experiences with "small deaths," examine how these can be used as "teachable moments," and provide guidelines for discussing death with children.

In the final chapter of Part A, Ellie Deveau begins with a review of children's cognitive development and how it relates to their perceptions of death. She examines the four subconcepts: universality, irreversibility, nonfunctionality, and causality and discusses the value of children and adolescents' artwork in relation to understanding their perceptions of death. Research findings are summarized and indicate the need for further investigation of the four subconcepts as well as consideration of other factors which may offer more information concerning how children acquire a mature understanding of death.

VOLUME 1–PART B:
The Influence of Society and Culture on Children and Adolescents' Perceptions and Attitudes Toward Life-Threatening Illness and Death

Although children and adolescents may have very limited or no direct experiences with death, the information presented in Part A of this volume clearly supports the fact that they still think about death. As children and teens contemplate this matter, many other variables concerning death-related issues enter their world transmitting both positive and negative information. The vulnerability, naivety, and inexperience of children may inhibit their ability to filter out negative, destructive information and retain information that will help them further their understanding of death-related issues. Children also incorporate the ideas, beliefs, and practices of parents and other significant adults in their lives and use these as a foundation for the development of their own beliefs and values. This being the case, encouraging children and adolescents to participate in the rituals of burial will promote involvement and provide additional information and experiences to help them round out their perceptions of, and attitudes toward, death.

In the first chapter, Hannelore Wass addresses the pervasive impact of violent death in popular culture. She examines the role of television, movies, music, and toys as learning grounds for violent acts which sensationalize death and threaten the value of human life. Wass supports Stillion's findings with regard to aggression in males, emphasizes the need to change public policy, and offers intervention guidelines for parents, teachers, and caregivers.

An interesting research study on American school age children's perceptions of the Persian Gulf War is presented by Gerry Cox, Bernie Vanden Berk, Ronald Fundis, and Patrick McGinnis. Their findings reveal age and gender differences in relation to children's feelings and attitudes about war and their tolerance of violence.

Robert Fulton discusses the results of an AIDS survey conducted with American university students. He challenges us as professionals and parents to view AIDS as an epidemic that adversely impacts on young people today and threatens future generations.

Does the culture, economy, and politics of a particular country play a critical role in the treatment of childhood cancer? Ida Martinson explores how these factors influence the adjustment, treatment, survival, and coping skills of children and families in four East Asian countries.

The last two chapters in this volume examine the role of funerals in children's understanding of death and adjustment to bereavement. Duane Weeks takes us back to a time when death was very much a part of children's lives and even young children participated in burial rituals. He stresses the importance of returning to the use of these rituals in today's society and provides specific tasks to facilitate children's participation in funeral ceremonies.

In the final chapter, Bunty Anderson responds to the question: Do children belong at funerals? She points out that children are disadvantaged grievers and discusses how funeral attendance provides them with a sense of belonging, allows them to commemorate their loss, and assists them in coping with their grief.

VOLUME 1–PART A

Children and Adolescents' Perceptions of Death

CHAPTER 1

Can You Answer Children's Questions?

Earl A. Grollman

> Nature constantly renews itself. It's the same for people. Living
> and dying are part of human unfolding [1, p. 42].

Children growing up today are all too aware of the reality of death,
perhaps more than adults realize. Even at a very young age, children
are confronted with that process when life no longer exists.

A pet is killed. A funeral procession passes by. A grandfather dies. A
leader is assassinated. And, of course, there is television with pictures
of death in living color.

Modern adults favor honesty when discussing the biological
process of birth with children. But when it comes to life's end,
health professionals, as well as parents, fall strangely silent
The feelings and perspectives of children are overlooked perhaps
because of denial, a belief that children cannot understand, fear
of the unknown, or simply a wish to escape this responsibility.

It has been my experience that many children were not even
told of the death of a family member! After all, the parents
were struggling with their own grief and could not possibly believe
that their children would understand such a tragic situation. However, silence only deprives children of the opportunity to share
their grief.

IF ADULTS ARE CONFUSED,
HOW CAN THEY HELP CHILDREN?

I know that I should discuss death with my children. But I'll be honest with you, I am confused myself. How would I begin? [1, p. 39].

Even adults do not understand the complete meaning of death. No mortal has ever pierced the veil of its great mystery. Professionals continue to wrestle with this thorny question as well. Yet, we have the inescapable responsibility of sharing with children the fragments of our experience and knowledge.

While insight is a gift, we must first place ourselves in a position to receive it. Children should be encouraged to tell *us* how *they* think, what *they* know, and where *they* need to go. We should respond by letting them know that we understand what they are trying to say. We should attempt to answer their questions in the spirit in which they were asked.

Adults trying to explain death to children are often tempted by half-truths or fantasies because they want to appear to know all the answers. We show our maturity when we say: "Are you surprised that I do not know everything about death? Don't be. Yet we can still talk about it. You can learn something from me. I can learn something from you. We can help each other."

CAN CHILDREN UNDERSTAND
THE MEANING OF DEATH?

The terms "dead" and "die" are common in young people's vocabulary. But these words conjure up divergent meanings.

Psychologist Maria Nagy, studying Hungarian children in the 1940s, discovered three phases in children's awareness of mortality [2]. She learned that children from three to five years of age may deny death as a regular and final process. To these children, death is like sleep; you are dead, then you are alive again. Or, it is like taking a journey; you are gone, then you come back again. Several times each day young children may experience some real aspects of what they consider to be "death," such as when their father goes to work and their mother goes to the supermarket.

Between five and nine years of age, children appear to be able to accept the idea that a person has died but may not understand it as something that will happen to everyone, and particularly to themselves. Around the ages of nine or ten, children recognize death as an inevitable experience that will occur even to them.

Of course, these are all rough approximations with many variations, but they prove to be valuable information for adults when children ask questions. Nagy's investigations also demonstrated the following recurring questions in children's minds: "What is death?" "What makes people die?" "What happens to people when they die?" "Where do they go?"

Kastenbaum tells us that adolescents, and even adults, have childlike views of death [3]. They "know" that death is inevitable and final, but most of their daily attitudes and actions are more consistent with the conviction that personal death is an unfounded rumor.

ARE FAIRY TALES A HELPFUL EXPLANATION FOR THE ENIGMA OF DEATH?

This question arises constantly: "What should we tell children when a death occurs?" Should we avoid acknowledging that the person has died? Should we suggest that a grandfather became ill and had to go away to a hospital where he could recuperate and become cured? This way the child's memory may gradually fade away and slowly he/she may come to accept grandfather's absence as being the norm.

It is far healthier to share the joint quest for wisdom with children than appease immediate curiosity with fantasy in the guise of fact. Evasions indicate that adults are uncertain about the child's capacity to deal with existing situations. It encourages the youngster to develop the capacity to "forget about things" and does not prepare him or her to deal with life's realities. We should never cover up with fiction that which we will some day repudiate. There is no greater need for children than trust and truth.

SHOULD CHILDREN BE DISCOURAGED FROM CRYING?

Why are you crying so hard? It's only a dog. It's not as if something happened to your parents. We can always buy another pet [1, p. 40].

Crying is a natural emotion. A newborn enters life crying for more oxygen. In early life, tears are an infant's means of expressing needs, pains, and discomforts. Even after children are able to verbalize their desires, they continue to weep in order to release painful emotions? When a pet dies, children come face to face with the real implications of death—its finality and the grief it brings. The special bond between a youngster and a pet is ended. For them, life is over. Weeping helps to express that inevitable depth of despair that follows the slow realization that the death is not a bad dream.

Adults should not feel as if they have failed when they weep in front of children. The opposite is true, for it expresses the undeniable fact that they too are human and need emotional release. It is better to say, "I could cry, too," rather than "There, you mustn't cry." Tears are wordless messages, a vital part of grieving for people of all ages.

HOW DO YOU TELL CHILDREN ABOUT THE DEATH OF SOMEONE CLOSE?

My daughter really surprised me when her grandmother died. She is such a tiny child, but she seemed more upset than most of the adults [1, p. 45].

It is important that children be informed *immediately*. If possible, they should be told by a parent or someone close to them. It is advisable to relay the sad news in familiar surroundings, preferably at home. Delay makes it all the more possible that children will be told of the death by the wrong person, at the wrong place, or in the wrong way.

There is no "right" or "proper" way. *What* is said is significant, but *how* it is said will have a greater bearing on whether youngsters develop unnecessary fears or will be able to accept, within their abilities, the reality of death. Approach children gently and with love. The tone of your voice—warm, sympathetic, and kind—will communicate feelings more completely than any specific words.

Stay close to children and let them feel your warmth and affection. Proceed gradually, according to their intellectual and emotional capabilities. Speak simply and accurately; be consistent in what you say. Do not overwhelm them with too much detail. Concepts about death should be translated into the language and comprehension level of the youngsters.

A FINAL THOUGHT

Talking about death is often a complex and disturbing task. In the end, of course, what we feel will determine what we teach children. If parents are overly disturbed by the thought of death, children will also feel their anxieties and tensions. Regardless of the language employed, emotional tones are transmitted.

The denial of death can lead us to the edge of the abyss and threaten our existence with meaninglessness and futility. Acceptance will help us and children start to build a bridge to span that chasm with the things of life that still count—memory, family, friendship, and love. Most important is the knowledge that life continues despite the pain. Grief is a strange mixture of joy and sorrow—joy to be alive and sorrow at having life diminished by the loss of a person we love.

REFERENCES

1. E. A. Grollman, *Talking About Death: A Dialogue Between Parent and Child*, Beacon Press, Boston, Massachusetts, 1970.
2. M. A. Nagy, The Child's Theories Concerning Death, *Journal of Genetic Psychology, 73*, pp. 2-27, 1948.
3. R. Kastenbaum, The Kingdom Where Nobody Dies, *Saturday Review, 56*, pp. 33-38, 1973.

BIBLIOGRAPHY

Feifel, H. (ed.), *The Meaning of Death*, McGraw-Hill, New York, 1959.

CHAPTER 2

Children and Death: Where Have We Been? Where Are We Now?

Charles A. Corr

TWO EXAMPLES OF UNSUCCESSFUL INTERACTIONS WITH CHILDREN ABOUT DEATH

First Example

Once upon a time, a colleague told me a true story about an incident during one summer when she took a class of students to Europe. She taught foreign languages and was eager for her students to spend some time experiencing the living language and culture of their classroom instruction. Each summer, she also took one of her children with her in order that they could become familiar with her native country, speak its language fluently, and spend time with their European relatives.

During the summer in question, my colleague invited her thirteen-year-old daughter to travel with her. One problem they faced was what to do with the daughter's pet hamster, which lived in a cage in her bedroom. Eventually, they decided to leave the hamster with the girl's grandmother who lived nearby. After returning from Europe, they brought the hamster home in its cage and everything seemed fine.

Soon thereafter, they discovered that the hamster was pregnant! This posed an interesting question: How did the hamster become pregnant alone in its cage?

In fact, the original hamster had died while the mother and daughter were gone. The grandmother had not wanted to admit this when they returned, so she bought another hamster that resembled the first one. Unfortunately, no one thought to check what the second hamster had been doing recently.

I suppose one moral that might be drawn from this story is that one need not confront death-related issues with children. In this case, however, that strategy raised even more perplexing questions about sexuality and reproduction. Clearly, a better lesson would have been to join with the child to address issues about death, dying, and bereavement. In that way, one would deal with life directly and would not get entangled in deception and more problems than had existed in the first place.

Second Example

Another example is found in the audiovisual, *And We Were Sad, Remember?* [1], which is part of the "Footsteps" series on parenting. This film is about the death of a grandmother and how both her children and her grandchildren cope with her death. In fact, her son, the father of two children, is not reacting very well to his mother's death. When the family gets together in his sister's home before the funeral, the father seems to be restless and unsettled. He is unable to stay in conversation with anyone and he is very uncomfortable talking about what has happened or about his own feelings.

At the same time, the children are playing with the girls' dolls in a bedroom. When they pretend that one of the dolls has died, one of the children wants to cover it with a blanket, but another child urges her not to do that because the blanket will prevent the "dead" doll from being able to breathe. That leads to an argument about whether individuals need to breathe after they die. In order to settle this argument, the children appeal to the first girl's father.

He does not want to talk about death and its implications. Instead, he sends all the children off to bed. But the oldest child is not to be put off so easily. She persists in asking him to agree that breathing stops with death. In his frustration and impatience, he replies: "Little girl, you don't have to worry about that for a hundred years."

I can imagine myself saying something like that in similar circumstances. But, of course, it is simply not true. It is not true that we do not have to worry about death for a hundred years or until the end of our lives. In fact, this little girl is dealing with death right now in the middle of her life—not her own death, but the death of her grandmother.

ADULTS, CHILDREN, AND DEATH:
PAST, PRESENT, AND FUTURE

Responsible adults should draw upon the breadth and depth of their own experiences in order to assist children to deal with death-related issues. They should not try to put children off until some later, supposedly safer, time. When Ross wrote that "a child is so recently of the quick that there is little need in his spring green world for an understanding of the dead" [2, p. 250], she was simply romanticizing childhood in an inaccurate and unhelpful way.

The goal of this chapter is to remind readers of where North American society was in the not-so-distant past in relationship to children and some selected death-related issues, to suggest where we have gone with these issues by the early 1990s, and to offer some suggestions for the future. It is always risky to try to speculate about the future, but perhaps some central directions can be identified in our progress from past to present and some guidelines can be inferred as we move from present to future.

CHILDREN AND DEATH

Children and their Encounters with Death

Let us begin by acknowledging that most children do encounter some forms of sadness, loss, and death in their lives. Many adults may agree with this statement when it is put so bluntly. But all too often, we behave as though this were not really true in practice—as if most children were really untouched by death. That led Kastenbaum to portray Edna St. Vincent Millay's description of childhood, "the kingdom where nobody dies," as "the fantasy of grown-ups" [3, p. 37].

All too often, adults project on to children a blissful ignorance, an absolute unawareness of issues related to death, dying, and bereavement. In fact, children encounter new events of all kinds. Death, and things that are related to death, are just some of these many new events experienced by children.

In response to their encounters, children are naturally inquisitive: "What is this?"; "What is it doing?" "What does it mean?" "Why are people reacting in the ways that they are?"

For many years, I have taught courses on "Children and Death" [4]. In these courses, I have asked countless college students to describe their earliest death-related experience. Nearly everyone can recall some death-related event from their childhood that stands out in their minds. It may not always have involved the death of a human being. Perhaps it was the death of a pet or an encounter with a dead wild animal. At the same time, those who remember such events can almost always remember what the adults around them did, and whether or not those adults were helpful during the experience.

The issue is not whether children will have death-related encounters, but whether adults will assist children to cope with their experiences and to integrate them into their lives in productive ways. What will adults do for, and with, children as they grapple with the realities of death, dying, and bereavement in their lives? Not to mention—What can adults learn from children about death?

Erikson wrote that "healthy children will not fear life if their elders have the integrity not to fear death" [5, p. 269]. Children do not necessarily fear everything that they encounter in life. Often, they are curious about life and wish to understand or make sense out of what it offers to them.

In the audiovisual, *The Day Grandpa Died* [6], a child comes home from school. As he enters the house, he yells, "Hi Mom, I'm home." Receiving no answer, he walks into the living room only to find his mother, his father, and another man (a rabbi). Everyone seems quite stiff; no one is moving. Naturally enough, the boy says, "What's wrong?" He senses that something is different, something has happened. The boy's father asks him to "come here" and says: "Last night your Grandpa went to sleep and he just never woke up." Immediately, the boy says, "He's dead!" Adults are deluding themselves when they act as if children have no experiences with, or awareness of, death.

In the United States in the most recent year for which reliable data are available (1991), approximately 37,000 infants under one year of age died each year, mainly as a result of congenital anomalies, Sudden Infant Death Syndrome, disorders relating to short gestation and unspecified low birthweight, and respiratory distress syndrome [7]. Their brothers and sisters experienced these deaths, together with the deaths of older children, peers, grandparents, parents, pets, and other animals.

Children, Death, and Its Significance for Them

In seeking to understand these experiences, it is important not to equate the significance of the death with external assessments of the intrinsic value of the object or person. I once observed to a class that the literature on death and dying, intended to be read by children, is largely focused on the deaths of pets or grandparents. I noted that publishers must see these as "safe" deaths. The people in the class said: "Safe for who?"

Is the death of a pet or grandparent a "safe" death for a child? Perhaps that pet is a source of security and affection for a child. Perhaps the grandparent had a very special relationship with the child. For many adults the death of a pet is not regarded as a very important event in life. Many adults perceive the death of an elderly person as an acceptable part of the natural order of things. People in other societies may not possess similar views. For example, the elder in a tribe might be regarded as its most important member because of his or her role as a repository of tribal wisdom and as a living connection with the history of the tribe.

It is important to assess the meaning of any death for the individual—adult or child—in question. In my family, the death of an elementary school janitor was a very significant event for our school-age children. They had no idea who the principal or district super-intendent was. They knew their own classroom teacher and a few other members of the teaching staff. But the janitor was the person who fixed the lights when the room got dark and scary. The janitor was the individual who shoveled the snow and helped them get in and out of the school in bad weather. In their eyes, the janitor was a very important person. He might not have had much status in society or even in the hierarchy of the school system. But he was rightly regarded as a figure of large significance by most of the children in his school building.

Most human deaths that children experience in early childhood probably relate to siblings or elderly adults. But that is not the entire story concerning encounters with death in early childhood. Things are different at different points throughout the remainder of childhood. This can be illustrated, perhaps most strikingly, by patterns of death-related encounters in adolescence in the United States [7, 8]. Here, the leading causes of death are accidents, homicide, and suicide. None of these are natural causes of death; all are human-induced deaths, deaths that we or other human beings have caused. Indeed, adolescence is the only developmental period in the life span in which there is no natural cause of death among the three leading causes of death. This is quite different from infancy or middle childhood. The important lesson here is to become sensitive to the developmental situation of each individual child in his or her maturation, just as it is critical to take into account the child's social circumstances and cultural context.

Children, Death, and the Societal Death System

Children from different ethnic groups, different social classes, and different parts of the world are likely to have varied types of encounters with death. This suggests that they may have different attitudes toward death and that the death-related practices with which they are familiar may also vary. Nevertheless, all children experience some death-related encounters, attitudes, and practices because they live within some type of societal death system [9].

In our society, it has been suggested that the death system tends to distance children from contact with natural human death. This has resulted from many factors: lower death rates and higher average life expectancy; different causes of death and longer, more ambiguous dying trajectories; a corresponding tendency to relocate many natural human deaths from the home and the mainstream of life into institutions; an inclination to transfer responsibilities of caring for the dying to professionals and specialists; and a similar trend to transfer responsibilities for handling and preparing the dead body by funeral industry personnel. Realistic experiences of natural human death that would have been typical in our society in a bygone era, and that are still typical in other social death systems elsewhere in the world, are being supplanted by unrealistic portrayals of death [10].

Children living in this type of a death system are not simply innocent of death and death-related events. In fact, the system sends them a number of messages about death, many of which suggest that it is not an appropriate subject for frank, everyday conversation. At the same time, there are many messages communicated to children which fantasize death. For example, children in our society are almost universally familiar with the "Road Runner" cartoon series in which Wyle E. Coyote "just keeps getting killed, but never really dies." And when Wyle is repeatedly subjected to deadly experiences, there is never time for bereavement, grief, or solace. Children may be expected to conclude that death is a temporary or transitory kind of thing which is not normally associated with tears or grief.

CHILDREN'S UNDERSTANDINGS OF DEATH

We should consider more directly the knowledge that children have in our society about death and the development of their death-related concepts. In this area, the classic text is an article published by Maria Nagy in the *Journal of Genetic Psychology* [11]. Nagy described a study that she undertook with children in Budapest just before the Second World War. She interviewed 378 children (51% boys, 49% girls) from three years old to a little over ten years old. The oldest children were asked to "write down everything that comes to your mind about death"; these children and some who were slightly younger were invited to draw pictures of death; and all of the children were interviewed, either to discuss their compositions and drawings, or to get them to talk about their ideas and feelings about death. In other words, this study employed different but overlapping methodologies.

As a result of her research, Nagy reported that she found three stages in the development of children's ideas about death. The first stage was that children did not understand death as final. They linked it to issues like sleep and travel. Dead persons were living elsewhere or they were living a diminished kind of life. Some adults appear to conclude from this that children in their early cognitive development do not yet have a concept of death. However, that is not correct. These children do have a concept of death, although it may not, as yet, be differentiated from other concepts. It also may be quite different from the types of concepts that many adults have of death.

In a second stage of development, Nagy maintained that children do conceptualize death as final, but they think of it as avoidable. That is, for those who die, they are dead and their lives are over and finished. However, one might avoid dying, if one does the right things.

In a third stage of development, Nagy reported that children understood death to be both final and not avoidable. In other words, death is universal and irreversible. It is an inescapable and internal part of human life.

This is an interesting and provocative study. Nagy identified many themes that are important in our understanding of death, themes such as finality, avoidability, universality, and internality. All of these are elements in various concepts of death. It is less clear that Nagy is correct in saying that all children develop in this way or that children of a certain chronological age are in a certain stage of cognitive development (i.e., Stage 1 = ages 3 to 5; Stage 2 = ages 5 to 9; and Stage 3 = ages 9 and above).

Many who have read Nagy's study have been especially attracted to this linkage between ages and stages. But cognitive development is not isomorphic to chronological age. Some children develop much more rapidly than others. Some children develop slowly. Some individuals who are chronologically adults remain at the level of children in their development. Children in different cultural or experiential contexts are in different situations.

It is comfortable for many people to fix children in age/stage categories. But that is oversimplified and risks stereotyping diverse individuals. Many limitations of this approach have been highlighted by the work of subsequent researchers [e.g., 12-15]. Another matter to consider: Is development a monolithic process? Is it like an elevator which moves upwards from one level to another? Or, is development much more complicated than this type of stage metaphor would imply?

DEVELOPMENT: BEYOND CHILDHOOD AND BEYOND COGNITION ALONE

In particular, I want to suggest that development is multidimensional and that it is affected by everything that goes on in the child's life. Intellects do not exist and develop on their own. They develop in the contexts of whole persons and their entire lives, including the influences that their environment has upon them. To understand children and their interactions with death in a comprehensive and responsible way, we certainly must pay attention to their developmental levels. But development is not merely a cognitive affair; it involves thoughts, feelings, behaviors, and values. Also, one must take into account life experiences, the personality of the individual child, and his or her patterns of communication [16].

Development Into and Within Adolescence

Further, we need to consider whether development stops at the pre-teen level. When children reach the age of ten, is their cognitive development complete? Do they now know about death and are they finished with that matter?

In Tolstoy's great novella, *The Death of Ivan Ilych*, Ivan is dying [17]. He is portrayed as a man in mid-life, someone who is successful in his career, has two children, is not very interested in his marriage, and plays cards with his friends. When Ivan discovers that he is dying, he also realizes that he is very much alone. No one really is willing to speak very candidly with him. One day he remembers what he had learned from a logic textbook: "All men are mortal, Caius is a man, therefore Caius is mortal." Up to that point, Ivan had thought, "Poor Caius" or "Poor humanity." Now, he realizes that this also applies to him.

Did Ivan have the capacity to understand the concept of death earlier than this? Certainly. Did he see that it related to him; that it had a personal significance? No. Should we focus exclusively on childhood and cognitive development or cognitive capacity, without attending to other issues, such as ongoing development and personal significance? [18, 19] Again, no; and we can explain why using the following four factors.

Development and Other Factors

1. *Self-Concept and Significance*

Ten years after Nagy's article, Alexander and Adlerstein reported a very interesting piece of research in the same journal [20]. These researchers conducted a word association test involving terms related to death, together with a measure of galvanic skin response. In these tests, slower responses and heightened conductivity were understood to be associated with higher levels of anxiety. The results in a population of 108 boys, five to sixteen years old, were displayed in a bimodal curve. That is, the results of this study appeared to display higher anxiety in five to eight-year-olds, lower anxiety in nine to twelve-year-olds, and increased anxiety in thirteen to sixteen-year-olds. The researchers concluded that individuals who have a more stable concept of self are less anxious about death, while those whose concepts of self are less stable are likely to be more anxious about death. The issue is not simply what one is capable of understanding about death. It is also at least an issue of what that understanding means to, and for, the particular child in question.

2. *Risk Perception and Risk Taking*

Another relevant piece of information comes from a Canadian transportation journal. Here Jonah studied risk-taking in adolescent drivers [21]. It is widely known that adolescent drivers take more risks than those in other age groups who drive. Why is this so? Jonah suggested that it has to do with two factors: 1) risk perception; and 2) risk utility. The first of these means that adolescent drivers may not perceive some of their behaviors to be as risky as they actually are, or as other drivers would perceive them to be. These adolescents may be relatively inexperienced as drivers, and thus underestimate the degree of risk inherent in their behaviors. Or, they may have great confidence in their invulnerability and fast reflexes, and thus minimize the personal danger in which they are placing themselves. The second factor—risk utility—suggests that adolescents may perceive that it is useful to take certain risks. For example, one may take risks to impress peers or to express strong emotions. Both of these factors, which bear upon risk-taking behavior in adolescent drivers, have to do not just with what the individual is intellectually capable of understanding but also with how the situation is interpreted and evaluated. The salient point is what the individual has learned from his or her life experiences and how the situation is related to his or her personal living.

3. Play

In terms of multidimensional aspects of development, Rochlin argued, based on his studies of children at play, that he could see in very young children strong feelings about death and strong death-related defenses [22]. In their games, such children kept death at a distance. Great violence was displayed, but it was kept within safe boundaries through the games and did not directly threaten children who controlled the games.

Similarly, Maurer argued that peek-a-boo is a death-related game in which it is the remainder of the world—not the egocentric child—that suddenly disappears and reappears in magical ways [23]. Others have noted that ring-around-the-rosy is a death-related chant arising from the little rosy pustules that one gets with smallpox and plague experiences in which "we all fall down."

4. The Lived Experience of Dying

In her study of *The Private Worlds of Dying Children*, Bluebond-Langner drew attention to the ways in which the significance of life experiences help children understand and interpret death [24]. She noted that the experience of dying was capable of altering the information which children acquired, as well as the ways in which they conceived their own self-concepts. At one point, Bluebond-Langner proposed that "all views of death . . . are present at all stages in one's development" [25, p. 51]. If adults were unaware of this, she suggested that adults either had not asked the right questions which would elicit such concepts or that adults had asked questions that yielded answers which were framed by the questions. One need not go quite this far to conclude that the life experiences of children influence and might accelerate their development.

Other publications in recent years have drawn attention to the spiritual lives of children [26] and to what spirituality and religious values may mean for bereaved children and adolescents [27].

HELPING CHILDREN COPE WITH DEATH: BEING EFFECTIVE IN PARENTING, TEACHING, COUNSELING, AND CAREGIVING

Death-related events and all of the "little deaths" throughout life have much to teach us about children, adolescents, coping, and communicating. For example, in a book by Corley, the children want to attend the funeral because they want to see the "polar bears" who carry the casket [28]. And in Agee's novel, *A Death in the Family*, a priest says to two children, "Your father died. He had an accident and God took him to heaven" [29]. Because the children understand an "accident" to refer to loss of bladder or bowel control, the message that they receive is that God seems to exact heavy penalties for such behavior. We may laugh at these examples, but they remind us of the need to speak clearly about death to children and adolescents, to attend to the ways in which messages are received, and to confirm what youngsters have (or have not) grasped from the communication.

Another example of important opportunities for interaction with children concerns "teachable moments" when life presents us with some events from which important lessons can be learned. Consider, for example, the situation of youngsters in school who were invited to watch the ascent of the Challenger space shuttle into space in 1986 because it had aboard a teacher from Massachusetts. When the shuttle exploded, perhaps no one was fully prepared to deal with that difficult situation. Surely, we knew prior to the explosion that this sort of travel into space was complicated and dangerous. But now the realities of what had happened had to be confronted, along with the strong reactions of viewers and (eventually) the grief of family members, friends, and all of the others who had participated in the launch. Educators and other adults who helped youngsters to understand, grieve, and commemorate this tragedy served children well and did not diminish the sad fact of the astronauts' deaths [30, 31].

COPING WITH THE REALITIES OF
LIFE AND DEATH

Katzenbach once made the following observations about children, fears, and the unknown:

> Do you know the sensation of being a child and being alone. Children can adapt wonderfully to specific fears like a pain, a sickness, or a death. It is the unknown which is truly terrifying to them. They have no fund of knowledge in how the world operates and so they feel completely vulnerable [32, p. 322].

Instead of leaving children alone and on their own to cope with fears, lack of knowledge, and vulnerability, Bruner has written that "any subject can be taught effectively in some intellectually honest form to any child at any stage of development" [33, p. 33]. The challenge is to identify what the child needs to learn and to determine how to satisfy those needs in an appropriate way. Some messages will inevitably be communicated. We cannot (and should not) keep children completely ignorant of all death-related events. Our choices are only how to interact with such children.

In order to help children to cope more effectively in the future with the realities of life and death, adults will need to become:

- more aware of the reality of death-related losses in the lives of children and adolescents;
- more sensitive to the many kinds of losses in the lives of children and adolescents;
- more appreciative of the differential impacts of different types of death-related experiences upon individual children and adolescents, and of the many varied responses made to such experiences by particular youngsters;
- more perceptive about the contexts within which death-related experiences are encountered, e.g., social, cultural, ethnic, and family systems;
- more critical of existing theoretical models that often have been taken for granted or applied uncritically to death-related experiences among children and adolescents;
- more responsive to the multiple dimensions and implications of development for coping with death throughout childhood and adolescence;
- more creative in developing new understandings of what death-related experiences mean for children and adolescents;
- more constructive in helping children and adolescents to cope with dying and bereavement;
- more respectful of the value of shared experiences for children and adolescents, e.g., shared with adults in funeral ritual and shared with other grieving youngsters in support groups;
- more open to learning from children and adolescents about death, dying, and bereavement.

These are things we can do and must do in order to secure a better future for children, adolescents, and ourselves.

REFERENCES

1. Northern Virginia Educational Telecommunications Association, *And We Were Sad, Remember?*, U-matic, color, 30 minutes, 1979. Available from the National Audiovisual Center, Reference Department, National Archives and Records Service, Washington, D.C., 20409.

2. E. S. Ross, Children's Books Relating to Death: A Discussion, in *Explaining Death to Children*, E. A. Grollman (ed.), Beacon Press, Boston, Massachusetts, pp. 249-271, 1967.
3. R. Kastenbaum, The Kingdom where Nobody Dies, *Saturday Review, 56*, January, pp. 33-38, 1973.
4. C. A. Corr, Teaching a College Course on Children and Death: A 13-year Report, *Death Studies, 16*, pp. 343-356, 1992.
5. E. H. Erikson, *Childhood and Society* (2nd Edition), W. W. Norton and Co., New York, 1963.
6. King Screen Productions, *The Day Grandpa Died*, 16mm film, 12 minutes, color, 1970. Available from King Screen Productions, 320 Aurora Avenue, North Seattle, Washington, 98109.
7. National Center for Health Statistics, Advance Report of Final Mortality Statistics, 1991, *Monthly Vital Statistics Report, 42*:8, Suppl., Public Health Service, Hyattsville, Maryland, 1993.
8. C. A. Corr, Understanding Adolescents and Death, in *Children and Death*, D. Papadatou and C. Papadatos (eds.), Hemisphere Publishing Corporation, New York, pp. 33-51, 1991.
9. R. Kastenbaum, On the Future of Death: Some Images and Options, *Omega, 3*, pp. 306-318, 1972.
10. C. A. Corr, C. M. Nabe, and D. M. Corr, *Death and Dying, Life and Living*, Brooks/Cole Publishing Company, Pacific Grove, California, 1994.
11. M. Nagy, The Child's Theories Concerning Death, *Journal of Genetic Psychology, 73*, pp. 3-27, 1948. Reprinted in *The Meaning of Death*, H. Feifel (ed.), McGraw-Hill, New York, pp. 79-98, 1959.
12. G. P. Koocher, Childhood, Death, and Cognitive Development, *Developmental Psychology, 9*, pp. 369-375, 1973.
13. A. Lazar and J. Torney-Purta, The Development of the Subconcepts of Death in Young Children: A Short-term Longitudinal Study, *Child Development, 62*, pp. 1321-1333, 1991.
14. R. Lonetto, *Children's Conceptions of Death*, Springer Publishing Company, New York, 1980.
15. H. Wass, Concepts of Death: A Developmental Perspective, in *Childhood and Death*, H. Wass and C. A. Corr (eds.), Hemisphere Publishing Corporation, New York, pp. 3-24, 1984.
16. R. Kastenbaum, Death and Development through the Lifespan, in *New Meanings of Death*, H. Feifel (ed.), McGraw-Hill, New York, pp. 17-45, 1977.
17. L. Tolstoy, *The Death of Ivan Ilych and Other Stories*, A. Maude (trans.), New American Library, New York, 1960. Original work published in 1884.
18. A. Maurer, Adolescent Attitudes toward Death, *Journal of Genetic Psychology, 105*, pp. 75-90, 1964.
19. L. D. Noppe and I. C. Noppe, Dialectical Themes in Adolescent Conceptions of Death, *Journal of Adolescent Research, 6*, pp. 28-42, 1991.

20. I. E. Alexander and A. M. Adlerstein, Affective Responses to the Concept of Death in a Population of Children and Early Adolescents, *Journal of Genetic Psychology, 83*, pp. 167-177, 1958.
21. B. A. Jonah, Accident Risk and Risk-taking Behaviour among Young Drivers, *Accident Analysis and Prevention, 18*:4, pp. 255-271, 1986.
22. G. Rochlin, How Younger Children View Death and Themselves, in *Explaining Death to Children*, E. A. Grollman (ed.), Beacon Press, Boston, Massachusetts, pp. 51-85, 1967.
23. A. Maurer, Maturation of the Conception of Death, *Journal of Medical Psychology, 39*, pp. 35-41, 1966.
24. M. Bluebond-Langner, *The Private Worlds of Dying Children*, Princeton University Press, Princeton, New Jersey, 1978.
25. M. Bluebond-Langner, Meanings of Death to Children, in *New Meanings of Death*, H. Feifel (ed.), McGraw-Hill, New York, pp. 47-66, 1977.
26. R. Coles, *The Spiritual Life of Children*, Houghton Mifflin, Boston, Massachusetts, 1990.
27. D. E. Balk, Sibling Death, Adolescent Bereavement, and Religion, *Death Studies, 15*, pp. 1-20, 1991.
28. E. A. Corley, *Tell Me about Death, Tell Me about Funerals*, Grammatical Sciences, Santa Clara, California, 1973.
29. J. Agee, *A Death in the Family*, Bantam, New York, 1969.
30. Anonymous, Children's Reactions to the Space Shuttle Tragedy, *Death Studies, 10*, pp. 491-505, 1986.
31. R. G. Stevenson, The Shuttle Tragedy, "Community Grief," and the Schools, *Death Studies, 10*, pp. 507-518, 1986.
32. J. Katzenbach, *The Traveler*, G. P. Putnam's Sons, New York, 1986.
33. J. S. Bruner, *The Process of Education*, Harvard University Press, Cambridge, Massachusetts, 1962.

CHAPTER 3

Gender Differences in Children's Understanding of Death

Judith M. Stillion

> Train up a child in the way he should go: and when he is old, he will
> not depart from it.
> — Proverbs, Chapter 22; Verse 6

Although there is a growing body of literature concerning children's understanding of death (i.e., over 80 studies have been documented [1]), there is a dearth of research which is systematically designed to examine gender differences in children's understanding of, and reaction to, death. Most of the studies that examine children's death concepts, death attitudes, or grief and coping behaviors do not report their results by sex. There are many reasons why this is so. First, researchers in the field of death and dying may be more interested in the commonalities of human reactions to various aspects of death than in differences by gender. Second, it is often difficult to obtain a large sample of children to participate in death related research because death is still a taboo topic and many parents refuse permission for their children to participate in such research [2, 3]. Therefore, samples may be too small to examine reliably by sex. Third, it simply may not occur to most researchers of children and death that gender is a salient factor that should be routinely examined when the size of sample permits. Whatever the reason, the result is that there are very few well-designed studies that examine gender differences in respect to death and childhood.

Because direct studies of gender differences in death issues are not available, this chapter will examine three separate streams of indirect information pertaining to death and coping with death that may shed

29

light on gender differences among children. The first is the statistical differential in the rates of death for males and females in utero, in infancy, and throughout childhood and adolescence. The second is research on traditional socialization of male and female children that may have implications for coping with death. Finally, one verified gender difference, aggression, which exists in early childhood and may partially account for the differential rates of death throughout child-hood and adolescence, will be examined in detail. The purpose of this chapter is to review briefly each of these major streams of information as they relate to possible sex differences in death attitudes and coping behaviors among children and to suggest implications of this material for parents, caregivers, and death educators.

THE FACTS OF DEATH FROM CONCEPTION THROUGH ADOLESCENCE

The gender differential in death is a reality in the worlds of humans from conception throughout life. Perhaps because the Y- (male) bearing sperm is smaller and faster, more males are conceived than females. An accepted estimate of the sex differential at conception is that 120 to 160 males are conceived for every 100 females [4, 5]. However, the male must undergo an additional process in order to experience masculiniza-tion. Between the sixth and twentieth weeks after conception, the male must begin production of testosterone. If this does not happen, the infant, although possessing the chromosomal make-up of a male (XY), will appear to be female. This extra step, resulting in a masculine organism existing in a feminine environment, may put the male at higher risk than the female fetus. An alternative explanation is that the male chromosome, because it carries less genetic information than the female chromosome, may predispose males to higher levels of pre-natal death. Whatever the cause, male embryos and fetuses die more often than do females so that at birth, there are only 106 males, out of the original 120 to 160 conceived, for every 100 live female births.

During the first year after birth the pattern continues with 20 percent more male than female deaths [6]. By the late teen years, the male advantage in numbers has been lost and females outnumber males across adulthood and into old age at increasing rates. Table 1 shows the average expectation of life in years for males and females in 1989, as well as the number of people surviving to specified ages per 1,000 born alive. It is clear that more females can expect to survive than males at every age indicated.

Table 2 adds an historical perspective to the facts of death by showing death rates by age, race, and sex across the last thirty years.

Table 1. Expectation of Life and Mortality Probabilities, 1989

| | Expectation of Life in Years | | | | | Mortality Probability per 1,000 | | | | |
| | Total Persons | White | | All Other | | Total Persons | White | | All Other | |
Age		Male	Female	Male	Female		Male	Female	Male	Female
0	75.3	72.7	79.2	67.1	75.2	9.9	9.1	7.2	17.6	15.0
1	75.0	72.3	78.8	67.3	75.4	0.7	0.7	0.5	1.1	0.9
2	74.1	71.4	77.8	66.4	74.4	0.5	0.5	0.4	0.8	0.7
3	73.1	70.4	76.9	65.5	73.5	0.4	0.4	0.3	0.7	0.6
4	72.1	69.5	75.9	64.5	72.5	0.3	0.3	0.3	0.5	0.5
5	71.1	68.5	74.9	63.5	71.6	0.3	0.3	0.2	0.5	0.4
6	70.2	67.5	73.9	62.6	70.6	0.2	0.3	0.2	0.4	0.3
7	69.2	66.5	73.0	61.6	69.6	0.2	0.3	0.2	0.4	0.3
8	68.2	65.5	72.0	60.6	68.6	0.2	0.2	0.2	0.3	0.2
9	67.2	64.5	71.0	59.6	67.6	0.2	0.2	0.2	0.3	0.2
10	66.2	63.6	70.0	58.6	66.6	0.2	0.2	0.1	0.2	0.2
11	65.2	62.6	69.0	57.7	65.7	0.2	0.2	0.1	0.2	0.2
12	64.3	61.6	68.0	56.7	64.7	0.2	0.2	0.2	0.3	0.3
13	63.3	60.6	67.0	55.7	63.7	0.3	0.4	0.2	0.5	0.3
14	62.3	59.6	66.0	54.7	62.7	0.5	0.6	0.3	0.8	0.3
15	61.3	58.6	65.1	53.8	61.7	0.6	0.8	0.4	1.1	0.4
16	60.4	57.7	64.1	52.8	60.8	0.8	1.0	0.5	1.3	0.4
17	59.4	56.8	63.1	51.9	59.8	0.9	0.2	0.5	1.6	0.5
18	58.5	55.8	62.1	51.0	58.8	1.0	1.3	0.6	1.9	0.5
19	57.5	54.9	61.2	50.1	57.8	1.0	1.4	0.5	2.1	0.6
20	56.6	54.0	60.2	49.2	56.9	1.1	1.4	0.5	2.3	0.7

Source: *Information Please Almanac Atlas and Yearbook* (46th Edition), Houghton Mifflin Company, Boston, 1993.

Table 2. Death Rates by Age, Race, and Sex

Males

Age	White Males 1990[a]	1989	1988	1980	1970[b]	1960	All Other Males 1990[a]	1989	1988	1980	1970[b]	1960
Under 1 year	9.0	9.0	9.3	12.3	21.1	26.9	15.3	19.1	18.9	23.5	40.2	51.9
1-4	0.4	0.4	0.5	0.7	0.8	1.0	0.6	0.8	0.7	1.0	1.4	2.1
5-14	0.2	0.2	0.2	0.4	0.5	0.5	0.3	0.3	0.3	0.4	0.6	0.8
15-24	1.4	1.3	1.3	1.7	1.7	1.4	2.2	2.1	2.0	2.0	3.0	2.1

Females

Age	White Females 1990[a]	1989	1988	1980	1970[b]	1960	All Other Females 1990[a]	1989	1988	1980	1970[b]	1960
Under 1 year	7.1	7.1	7.2	9.6	16.1	20.1	12.7	16.2	16.0	19.4	31.7	40.7
1-4	0.3	0.3	0.4	0.5	0.8	0.9	0.5	0.6	0.6	0.8	1.2	1.7
5-14	0.1	0.1	0.1	0.2	0.3	0.3	0.2	0.2	0.2	0.3	0.4	0.5
15-24	0.4	0.4	0.4	0.5	0.6	0.5	0.6	0.6	0.6	0.7	1.1	1.1

[a]Provisional based on a 10 percent sample of deaths.
[b]Beginning 1970 excludes deaths of nonresidents of the United States.
Note: Excludes fetal deaths. Rates are per 1,000 population in each group, enumerated as of April 1 for 1960, 1970, and 1980, and estimated as of July 1 for all other years.
Sources: Department of Health and Human Services, National Center for Health Statistics.

Clearly, impressive gains have been made in decreasing death rates across that period, but males remain at higher risk for death than females throughout childhood and adolescence.

We can do little or nothing at present to alter the genetic inheritance or the pre-natal environment of boys and girls. Male children seem destined to die at higher numbers from conception throughout the pre-natal period. However, we can examine the post-natal environment as well as our socialization practices to see if we are systematically predisposing male children to higher risks of death than we do our female children.

DIFFERENTIAL SOCIALIZATION

Humans in all societies tend to socialize males and females differently [7]. The socialization process begins as soon as the sex of the baby is known, perhaps before birth. Studies have shown that adults react differently to babies based on their understanding of the child's sex [8, 9]. Boys are handled more roughly; girls are spoken to in gentler tones. Boys are placed in rooms decorated with sports scenes or cars in bright colors, while girls tend to be placed in pink and white lace-filled rooms. In this way, children draw, from their surroundings and the people around them, a basic understanding of who they are and the way they should interact with their environment.

Furthermore, physical sex is a basic tool by which children organize their understandings of the world. Kohlberg suggested that children develop their basic gender identity (i.e., the knowledge that they are a boy or a girl) within the first year [10]. During the next four years they develop the concept of gender stability (i.e., the knowledge that their gender identity will not change across their lifetimes), and gender constancy (i.e., recognition that gender remains constant even if boys have long hair or girls wear denims and play football). Like a rolling snowball, growing larger and more solid as it moves along, children use these core understandings about gender actively as salient factors in organizing their worlds. Thus, by the time children reach school age they have entered sex-typed worlds and are knowledgeable about, and comfortable with, gender role stereotypes.

In contemporary western society, we have traditionally socialized males to be "more independent, assertive, dominant, and competitive" than females, while we have stressed that females should be "more passive, loving, sensitive, and supportive in social relationships" [7, p. 533]. In spite of some pressure to change or at least loosen gender roles, these traits have remained constant across the last twenty years [11] and have been found to hold true across twenty-five different cultures [12]. Girls are also expected to express more warmth and nurturance in personal relationships and more anxiety under pressure, while boys are taught to control emotional expression and to deny anxiety. One study has shown that by eleven years of age, females admit to experiencing a higher incidence of frightening dreams and of being more afraid at bedtime than their male counterparts [13]. Although we found no definitive studies documenting sex differences in death anxiety in young children, this early tendency for females to admit anxiety more than males may presage the research. Much of the research, carried out with college-age students, consistently shows that females admit to higher death anxiety than males [14-17]. Thus, differential socialization in expressiveness may permit female children to admit fears, discuss them with significant others, and be comforted more easily than male children. Male children, on the other hand, living up to the norm of independence and emotional toughness, may repress emotions connected with death. They may use denial or substitution of activity to deal with the free-floating anxiety that arises when the subject is raised.

Children experience deaths of significant others throughout their childhood. Once again, there is a paucity of literature examining male-female differences in coping during childhood. However, one recent study did examine gender differences in coping with the death of a parent [18]. While there was no significant difference by sex in immediate methods of coping with the death, the authors noted the following in their discussion of the findings:

> Boys, especially the older ones, were less comfortable with their feelings and were more likely to get reinforcement from their support network to contain their feelings. This finding raises the question of whether these boys were already being socialized, at this early age, to perpetuate the pattern of the larger society in which women deal with the feelings in the family [18, p. 102].

Another study documented that bereaved boys had more school impairment than did bereaved girls [19]. Finally, an older study, that examined males who were institutionalized and diagnosed as highly depressed, found that 37.8 percent had lost a parent before sixteen years of age. The corresponding figure for women who were highly depressed was 25.4 percent [20]. This preliminary evidence, weak and unreplicated as it is, might lead us to hypothesize that male socialization toward emotional inexpressiveness is one factor that causes higher levels of poor ability to cope with death among male children. However, this hypothesis needs to be systematically examined in a series of studies designed specifically to assess gender differences among bereaved children.

In addition to experiencing the death of significant others, at some point in childhood, children become familiar with the subject of suicide. Sex differences in child and adolescent suicide have been documented throughout this century. Males at every age are more likely to die from suicide than are females, but adolescent females are far more likely to make suicide attempts than are males. In an attempt to understand how young people view suicide, a series of studies, begun in the early 1980s, has been carried out by the author and her associates. Utilizing young people between the ages of fourteen and twenty-one, these researchers established, in seven different studies, that females tend to be more sympathetic to young people who attempt suicide than do males [21-24]. In addition, males tend to sympathize far less with males who attempt suicide than they do with troubled males who do not attempt suicide, or with females in either condition [25]. This fact seems to indicate that males reject other males who react to stress with what they may consider to be weakness.

Although the evidence is scanty at present, it would seem that the socialization of males encourages them to be less open in their emotions and less able to admit to being anxious as well as less likely to sympathize with suicidal figures in vignettes. In addition, they seem to make harsher judgments of males who use suicide attempts as a method of coping than they do of the same males in the same situations who do not attempt suicide. Females, on the other hand, are more likely to express their feelings, including feelings of sympathy for suicidal figures and feelings of fear and death anxiety. These findings might be considered to be harmless gender differences if they existed in a vacuum. However, the fact is that they exist in an era in which males can expect to die seven years before females and in a time when death by violence is an increasingly familiar reality, especially for males in western culture. Could it be that the socialization pressures we have examined, perhaps building upon a basic biological predisposition to earlier male death, might be involved in the differential longevity figures of male and female children? To shed some light on that question, we should look in more depth at one final gender difference, aggression, which may illuminate the excess of male deaths across childhood and adolescence.

GENDER DIFFERENCES IN AGGRESSION

Aggression, defined as behavior that intentionally harms or injures another person, is a key element in violence. As early as researchers have been able to measure it, there has been a consistent gender difference in aggression levels [26-28]. Studies of pre-school children have shown that boys more often than girls: exhibit aggressive behaviors; are more likely to react aggressively when attacked; and approve more of aggression [28, 29]. Moreover, a sex difference in aggression has been found in most mammalian species [30]. All of these studies taken together might suggest that there is a biological basis to aggressive behavior.

However, most investigators believe that aggression is a malleable behavior that can be inhibited or exhibited depending upon the conditions and expectations dominant in the environment [30]. The environment of the late twentieth century in the United States appears to be one that encourages, fosters, and rewards children's, especially male children's, expression of aggression. A brief examination of only three elements of socialization, that is, television, music, and toys and games, will make the point.

Two classic reports on television, spaced a decade apart, point to the role of televised violence in predisposing children, especially male children, to violence [31, 32]. Furthermore, the cover of a recent issue of *Newsweek* was devoted to the topic of children and aggression. This issue entitled, "Growing Up Scared: How our Kids are robbed of their Childhood," documented that the "average child has watched 8,000 televised murders and 100,000 acts of violence before finishing elementary school" [33, p. 44]. It cited FBI crime reports as stating that "children under 18 are 244 percent more likely to be killed by guns than they were in 1986" [33, p. 44]. In effect, we have been conducting a huge social experiment across the last several decades. We have conclusively shown that exposing children to violence accelerates violence in their personal behaviors and leads to a more violent world. Thus, it should not be surprising to note that "one in six youths between the ages of 10 and 17 has seen or knows someone who has been shot" [33, p. 44].

With regard to music, Wass and Miller state that adolescents in grades seven through twelve spend an estimated 10,500 hours listening to rock music [34]. Furthermore, Wass has pointed out that since the 1980s the character of lyrics within rock music has changed appreciably [35]. Some of the heavy metal and rap music specifically promote hatred, violence, and murder. Wass estimates that nearly a fifth of those young people who listen to this type of music report themselves to be fans of the more destructive and violent lyrics and groups. In a large sample of students (894) enrolled in grades nine through twelve, investigators found that males were significantly more likely than females to be fans of rock music with lyrics that promote suicide, homicide, or satanic practices [34, 35].

Even a cursory look at children's toys and games indicates that males spend more time than females entertaining themselves with violent themes from "Cowboys and Indians" to "Army." Little boys begin to say, "Bang, bang, you're dead!" almost as early as they can talk. Carlsson-Paige and Levin have reported that the sale of war toys has risen approximately 500 percent between 1984 and 1990 [36]. As children enter school, organized games, primarily designed for male children, stress competition (e.g., T-ball) and reward aggression (e.g., football). Consequently, by the time children reach the age of seven years, boys prefer playing with guns, engaging in active aggressive play such as wrestling and karate, and taking part in competitive team sports. On the other hand, girls prefer playing with dolls, cooking, reading, and caring for children [37]. Tolerance and even encouragement of these trends, by adults and peers, make such choices appear to be "normal." Therefore, by age six, children's understanding of the way they should behave in order to be accepted as male or female has been shaped. Boys expect the world to be more violent than girls do and each gender acts on its assumptions, thus, to some extent at least, bringing about a self-fulfilling prophecy.

We have seen that males die more often from almost all causes of death throughout childhood. However, there are three causes of death that deserve special attention because of their preventability, as well as the large sex difference in childhood deaths: accidents, suicide, and homicide. Aggression and violence form the core of suicidal and homicidal behavior and are also contributing factors in many deaths by accident.

Table 3 shows that males are more than twice as likely as females to die from accidents between the ages of one and fourteen and more than three times as likely to die accidentally between fifteen and twenty-four years of age. Many accidents result from males' attempts to be true to the stereotypical male role: to be adventurous, brave, and daring; to deny fear; and, in the current vernacular, to "push the envelope." Many accidental deaths are from gunshot wounds and boys are from three to ten times more likely to die from accidental gunshot wounds, depending on age, than are girls [38]. Since guns are inherently aggressive instruments, this figure probably reflects boys' greater fascination with tools of aggression.

Homicide claims nearly twice as many boys as girls across the years of childhood and adolescence. It is the fourth leading cause of death among children between the ages of one and fourteen and the second leading cause of death among young people fifteen to twenty-four years of age. Table 3 shows that white males between the ages of fifteen and twenty-four are almost four times more likely to be murdered than are

Table 3. Rates of Death by Sex, Race, and Age in the United States, 1992

Cause of Death	Under 1 Year				1-14 Years				15-24 Years			
	White		Black		White		Black		White		Black	
	Male	Female	Male	Female	Male	Female	Male	Female	Male	Female	Male	Female
Accidents	18.0	18.3	34.0	38.0	14.2	6.5	19.4	12.4	59.9	19.6	44.4	16.5
Suicide	—	—	—	—	1.0	B	B	B	4.1	4.1	17.3	B
Homicide	7.4	B	B	B	1.6	1.3	6.2	3.8	16.1	4.8	161.1	23.2

Note: B = base figure too small to meet statistical standards for reliability of a desired figure.
Source: National Center for Death Statistics, U.S. Department of Health and Human Services.

38

their female peers, while black males are nearly seven times more likely to be murdered than are black females. Furthermore, males are more likely to kill than are females. This is true across cultures and across time [16]. Although the thrust of this chapter is on sex differences, no discussion of homicide among children would be complete if it did not note the extreme racial differences in homicide in the United States. Just as males live in more violent worlds than females, African American children live in far more violent worlds than white children. Indeed, homicide has been the leading cause of death among African American males for over a decade [39] and black males are over ten times as likely to be killed as white males [35].

Suicide shows an even more remarkable gender difference, causing almost three times as many male as female deaths between the age of one and fourteen years and over six times as many male as female deaths between fifteen and twenty-four years of age [38]. It is clear from statistics on accidents, homicide, and suicide that males live in more violent worlds than females do and that a significant amount of the sex differential in longevity is caused by the difference in death by violence among male and female children.

IMPLICATIONS FOR PARENTS AND INTERESTED ADULTS

We do not have to continue to socialize males to live in more violent worlds, to be emotionally inexpressive, and ultimately to die prematurely. Bernard observed over a decade ago that male socialization is malleable. She stated:

> Presented only as food for thought, and certainly not as a hypothesis, is the idea that just as the primordial fetal stuff would remain female if not prodded by the male hormone, so the "real" nature of humanity or "human nature" would probably be more like "female" human nature than like the nature that has to be achieved with so much effort as "male" nature is, if it were not prodded from infancy on to be aggressive, competitive, dominant [40, p. 544].

More recently, Lore and Schultz suggested relatively simple changes that could be made to decrease violent death in our society, including endorsing a national policy that discourages the expression of individual aggression, adopts a more stringent gun control, and limits "the almost continuous exposure to glorified, unrealistic violence in the entertainment media" [30, p. 23].

In addition, Hetherington and Parke have reported on a program instituted in schools in Norway and Sweden that was successful in bringing about "marked reductions in the levels of aggression problems both eight and twenty months after the initiation of the intervention program" [7, p. 604]. This program targeted teachers, parents, and children seeking to increase awareness of the scope of the aggressive behavior in the schools, to involve parents and teachers in direct action against such aggression, to develop clear rules against aggressive behavior, and to provide support for victims of aggression [7]. Such programs are evidence that the first thing necessary for a society to change the frequency of death by violence is recognition of the problem and specific determination to make such behavior unacceptable.

In a more general sense, however, what is needed is an awareness that current socialization processes, perhaps building upon genetically determined and biologically, as well as socially reinforced tendencies, are placing our male children at higher risk than our female children. If we want to achieve true equality of opportunity in the realm of life expectancy, rational adults, cognizant of the statistical differential in death between the sexes in childhood, must begin to reassess the way we socialize our children. Beginning with a new definition of what it means to be a mature adult, one which discounts aggression and violence and emphasizes productivity in work and relationships, we must start to hold parents, schools, and the media responsible for the messages they give our children. Males and females alike should be encouraged by every facet of society to develop positive coping skills and good interpersonal communication, and to set positive personal goals for their lives. Negative models, utilizing violence to achieve their ends, should disappear from entertainment media. Caring adults should demand that the world of children be made safer by controlling the number of guns available in their worlds. The messages given to both male and female children should be unanimous in asserting the value of human life and individual responsibility, in promoting positive expression of feeling, and in reinforcing the power of nurturance. Our society remains convinced of the truth of the statement cited at the beginning of this chapter; early socialization has lasting effects on children. Perhaps it is time that we systematically revise the ways in which we are socializing our children so that more of them become competent adults who inhabit a significantly safer world and are able to deal with fear of death and loss in positive ways. If responsible adults confront these issues today, perhaps future children, both males and females, will realize the ultimate in equal opportunity; the opportunity to realize their life expectancy.

REFERENCES

1. S. B. Brent and M. W. Speece, "Adult" Conceptualization of Irreversibility: Implications for the Development of the Concept of Death, *Death Studies, 17*, pp. 203-224, 1993.

2. K. Townley and K. R. Thornburg, Maturation of the Concept of Death in Elementary School Children, *Educational Research Quarterly, 5*, pp. 17-24, 1980.

3. A. Lazar and J. Torney-Purta, The Development of the Sub-Concepts of Death in Young Children: A Short-Term Longitudinal Study, *Child Development, 62*, pp. 1321-1333, 1991.

4. M. Ounsted, Gender and Intrauterine Growth with a Note on the Use of the Sex Proband as a Research Tool, in *Gender Differences: Their Ontogeny and Significance,* C. Armisted and D. C. Taylor (eds.), Churchill Livingston, London, pp. 177-201, 1972.

5. U. Tricomi, D. Serr, and G. Solish, The Ratio of Male to Female Embryos as Determined by the Sex Chromatin, *American Journal of Obstetrics and Gynecology, 79*, pp. 504-509, 1960.

6. U.S. Bureau of the Census, *Statistical Abstract of the United States: 1992* (112th Edition), Washington, D.C., 1992.

7. E. M. Hetherington and R. D. Parke, *Child Psychology: A Contemporary Viewpoint* (4th Edition), McGraw-Hill, Inc., New York, 1993.

8. J. Z. Rubin, F. J. Provenzano, and A. Luria, The Eye of the Beholder: Parents' Views on Sex of Newborns, *American Journal of Orthopsychiatry, 43*, pp. 720-731, 1974.

9. M. Stern and K. H. Karraker, Sex Stereotyping of Infants: A Review of Gender Labeling Studies, *Sex Roles, 20,* pp. 501-522, 1989.

10. L. A. Kohlberg, A Cognitive-Developmental Analysis of Children's Sex-role Concepts and Attitudes, in *The Development of Sex Differences*, E. E. Maccoby (ed.), Stanford University Press, pp. 82-173, 1966.

11. D. J. Bergen and J. E. Williams, Sex Stereotypes in the United States Revisited: 1972-1988, *Sex Roles, 24*, pp. 413-423, 1991.

12. J. E. Williams and D. L. Best, *Measuring Sex Stereotypes: A Multinational Study*, Sage, Newbury Park, California, 1990.

13. D. Bauer, An Exploratory Study of Developmental Changes in Children's Fears, *Journal of Child Psychiatry, 17,* pp. 69-74, 1976.

14. D. I. Templer, C. F. Ruff, and C. M. Franks, Death Anxiety: Age, Sex, and Parental Resemblance in Diverse Populations, *Developmental Psychology, 4,* p. 108, 1971.

15. D. I. Templer, D. Lester, and C. F. Ruff, Fear of Death and Femininity, *Psychological Reports, 35,* p. 530, 1974.

16. J. M. Stillion, *Death and the Sexes: An Examination of Differential Longevity, Attitudes, Behaviors and Coping Skills*, Hemisphere/McGraw-Hill International, New York, 1985.

17. D. Lester, The Fear of Death, Sex and Androgyny, *Omega, 15*, pp. 271-274, 1985.

18. P. R. Silverman and J. W. Worden, Children's Reactions in the Early Months after the Death of a Parent, *American Journal of Orthopsychiatry, 62*, pp. 93-104, 1992.
19. M. A. Fristad, R. Jedel, R. A. Weller, and E. G. Weller, Psychosocial Functioning in Children after the Death of a Parent, *American Journal of Psychiatry, 150*, pp. 511-513, 1993.
20. A. Beck, B. Sethi, and R. Tuthill, Childhood Bereavement and Adult Depression, *Archives of General Psychiatry, 9*, pp. 295-336, 1963.
21. J. M. Stillion, E. E. McDowell, and J. B. Shamblin, The Suicide Attitude Vignette Experience: A Method for Measuring Adolescent Attitudes Toward Suicide, *Death Studies, 8*, pp. 65-80, 1984.
22. J. M. Stillion, E. E. McDowell, and J. May, Developmental Trends and Sex Differences in Adolescent Attitudes Toward Suicide, *Death Studies, 8*, pp. 81-90, 1984.
23. J. M. Stillion, E. E. McDowell, R. T. Smith, and P. A. McCoy, Relationships Between Suicide Attitudes and Indicators of Mental Health Among Adolescents, *Death Studies, 10*, pp. 289-296, 1986.
24. J. M. Stillion, H. White, E. E. McDowell, and P. J. Edwards, Ageism and Sexism in Suicide Attitudes, *Death Studies, 13*, pp. 247-261, 1989.
25. H. White and J. M. Stillion, Sex Differences in Attitudes Toward Suicide, *Psychology of Women Quarterly, 12*, pp. 357-366, 1988.
26. E. E. Maccoby and C. N. Jacklin, *The Psychology of Sex Differences*, Stanford University Press, Stanford, California, 1974.
27. E. E. Maccoby and C. N. Jacklin, Sex Differences in Aggression: A Rejoinder and Reprise, *Child Development, 51*, pp. 964-980, 1980.
28. D. G. Perry, L. C. Perry, and J. P. Boldizar, Learning of Aggression, in *Handbook of Developmental Psychopathology*, M. Lewis and S. M. Miller (eds.), Plenum, New York, pp. 135-146, 1990.
29. L. R. Huesmann, N. G. Guerra, A. Zeilli, and L. Miller, Differing Normative Beliefs about Boys and Girls, in *Of Mice and Women: Aspects of Female Aggression*, K. Bjorkquist and P. Niemele (eds.), Academic Press, Orlando, Florida, pp. 77-87, 1992.
30. R. K. Lore and L. A. Schultz, Control of Human Aggression: A Comparative Perspective, *American Psychologist, 48*, pp. 16-25, 1993.
31. Surgeon General's Scientific Advisory Committee Report on Television and Social Behavior, *Television and Growing Up: The Impact of Televised Violence*, U.S. Government Printing Office, Washington, D.C., 1972.
32. D. Pearl, L. Bouthilet, and J. Lazar, *Television and Behavior: Ten Years of Scientific Progress and Implications for the Eighties*, U.S. Government Printing Office, Washington, D.C., 1982.
33. J. Adler, Kids Growing Up Scared, *Newsweek*, pp. 43-49, January 10, 1994.
34. H. Wass and M. D. Miller, Factors Affecting Adolescents' Behavior and Attitudes Toward Destructive Rock Lyrics, *Death Studies, 13*, pp. 287-303, 1989.

35. H. Wass, Death in the Lives of Children and Adolescents, in *Dying: Facing the Facts* (3rd Edition), H. Wass and R. Neimeyer (eds.), Taylor and Francis, New York, 1995.
36. N. Carlsson-Paige and D. E. Levin, *Who's Calling the Shots: How to Respond Effectively to Children's Fascination with War Play and War Toys*, New Society Publishers, Philadelphia, 1990.
37. N. Zill, *Happy, Healthy, and Insecure*, Cambridge University Press, New York, 1986.
38. National Center for Health Statistics, Annual Summary of Births, Marriages, Divorces, and Deaths: United States, 1992, *Monthly Vital Statistics Report, 41*, Public Health Service, Hyattsville, Maryland, p. 13, 1993.
39. W. R. Hammond and B. Yung, Psychology's Role in the Public Health Response to Assaultive Violence Among Young Afro-American Men, *American Psychologist, 48*, pp. 142-154, 1993.
40. J. Bernard, *The Female World*, The Free Press, New York, 1981.

CHAPTER 4

Using Life Experiences as a Way of Helping Children Understand Death

Lynne Ann DeSpelder and Albert Lee Strickland

A child encounters a dead bird while out for a walk. In the garden or the classroom, a plant gets too much sunlight and begins to wither and die. News reports give prominent coverage to the unexpected death of a popular celebrity, sports idol, or political figure. In various contexts and circumstances, death becomes part of children's lives. This encounter sets them off on personal voyages of discovery to learn both the facts of death and its meaning. Parents, along with other adults including educators and child-care professionals, have significant roles to play in assisting children on their journeys toward understanding the place of death in human experience.

Throughout childhood, children experience various "small deaths" that occur with separations from toys, pets, and people [1]. They find portrayals of loss and grief in fairy tales and stories, as well as in television programs and movies. In their efforts to understand death, children draw upon a variety of sources for both information and example. These sources include parental messages (both explicit and unintentional), cultural influences, and their own life experiences.

Even young children possess some understanding about the facts of death and the limits and uncertainty of life [2]. Robert Kastenbaum observes that "thoughts about death are intertwined with the total pattern of personality development right from the beginning, influencing and being influenced by all the child's experiences" [3, p. 106]. For children, as for adults, learning about death is not something that is odd or extraordinary; it is simply learning about life [4].

USING TEACHABLE MOMENTS

Through the normal course of life, opportunities abound for helping children learn about dying and death. Consider, for example, a mother who discovers her eleven-year-old son sitting at her new computer writing his will. Taken aback, she pauses for a moment as these questions race through her head: Why is he writing a will? How did an eleven-year-old become interested in giving away his favorite treasures? Does he believe he is going to die soon? What should I do? What can I say? Gathering her courage, she cautiously adjusts her tone to suggest a neutral inquisitiveness and asks, "What has made you think about writing a will?" Turning to her, the joy of accomplishment lighting up his face, the boy says, "I was looking at the menu on your computer and found *Willmaker 5*. The program came up and all I have to do is fill in the blanks. It's easy, see? Then I can print out my very own will."

Thus we encounter the concept of a "teachable moment," a phrase used by educators to describe opportunities for learning that arise out of ordinary experiences. Because of their immediacy, such naturally occurring events are ideal vehicles for learning [5]. The learner's own questions, enthusiasm, and motivation guide and become integral to the educational process [6]. Such involvement leads to powerful and appropriate learning [7]. When parents and other adults recognize and make use of the opportunities presented by teachable moments, children are able to learn about death in a natural and non-threatening way.

Using teachable moments to enhance learning is appropriate in various settings and among diverse age groups. In hospitals, practitioners find that hospitalization itself is a teachable moment for prompting patients to quit smoking [8]. A senior center in Montreal uses teachable moments in adult education for the elderly [9]. Home energy conservation has been promoted by using teachable moments to capitalize on the interests and needs of home-owners and to design school programs that encourage learning transfer from children to parents [10]. In peer-based HIV risk assessment among college-age youth, the use of teachable moments is at the center of an educational process which occurs at unscheduled times within the informal context of students' natural interactions with one another [11]. Among members of a Canadian gymnastics team, the systematic use of teachable moments proved to be helpful and effective during training as well as Olympic competition [12].

Teachable moments have been defined as "unanticipated events in life that offer potential for developing useful educational insights and lessons, as well as for personal growth" [13, p. 457]. This is a useful definition, but it requires expansion. We need to beware of several assumptions that may be made unwittingly if our understanding of teachable moments is limited to this definition.

EXAMINING ASSUMPTIONS

First, we must determine who is the teacher. If we assume that learning about death always flows in a single direction, from adult to child, we overlook the quintessential quality of education as an interactive process. In the foregoing example of the young boy filling in the blanks of a computerized will-making program, the mother appears to occupy most clearly the role of the student. She learns something about her son's exploration of the new computer and, more important, she learns the crucial lesson of gathering information before reacting.

Suppose this mother, acting out of initial shock at her son's apparent interest in death, had hastily responded, "Stop that! Children shouldn't be thinking about wills or about dying!" A lesson about death would surely be taught, but it would not promote a healthy understanding of death. So, in thinking about how to apply the concept of teachable moments to help children understand death, it is useful to ask: *"What* is being taught?" "Does the 'teaching' result from a conscious design, or, is it unintentionally conveying unhealthy messages about death?" To use ordinary life experiences in helping children grow in their understanding of death, we need to consider our aims and purposes. What outcome do we wish to achieve?

Let us return to our story of the mother and son. Having elicited information from her child and refrained from acting on her initial fears, the mother was able to use this interchange with her son as a teachable moment, an opportunity to discuss death in a nonthreatening and unemotional context. She may proceed to broach the subject by calling her son's attention to the entry for "Designated Guardian for Minor Children," thereby taking advantage of the opportunity to inform him about the steps she has taken to ensure his well-being ("Did I tell you that I listed Aunt Martha and Uncle John as your guardians in my will?"). In addition, she may respond to any of his concerns ("No, I do not intend to die for a long time"). They might spend a few minutes discussing other aspects of death and how people prepare for it. In a brief conversation, considerable learning can take place. An atmosphere of openness in talking about death is promoted as information is exchanged between adult and child. Death becomes something that can be discussed in a non-threatening context as a normal part of life.

In this example, the event that prompted the discussion of death was unanticipated. Although teachable moments are often defined in the context of unplanned or unexpected occurrences, it is useful to recognize that parents, educators, and other adults can consciously create situations that encourage such learning opportunities [14]. There is no rule specifying that we must wait until such events happen spontaneously. Indeed, in the foregoing example, the mother made use of her son's experience with the computer program as a way of introducing their subsequent discussion about death.

Children are exposed to events of loss and death through stories, television programs, and other similar avenues. Adults can guide children's interest toward stories or programs that deal with death in a manner appropriate for their age and understanding. Creating such informal learning situations opens up the possibility for teachable moments to grow naturally out of children's interests and concerns. The key to capitalizing on such occurrences involves adequate preparation by trusted adults in the child's environment.

PREPARING TO DISCUSS DEATH
WITH CHILDREN

Edgar Jackson points out that "every death experience for a child can be a learning opportunity. Death is so much a part of the life of a child that it is imperative that it be dealt with in positive ways" [15, p. 37]. As with most activities in life, successful interactions with children around issues involving dying or death result from adequate and thoughtful preparation. Such preparation is twofold: 1) attending to our own feelings and thoughts about death so that we become more conscious of them; and 2) pursuing whatever study is needed so that we can respond appropriately to children's questions and concerns.

As for the first element in preparing ourselves to make use of opportunities to discuss death with children, we should recognize that "without an examination of our own feelings and attitudes about death, we are likely to misunderstand a child's questions and concerns or to make an incorrect assumption of how to help" [16, p. 6]. Self-examination helps us become aware of the fact that, even as adults, we do not possess all the answers about death. Indeed, if we are psychologically alive, we continue to modify our orientation toward death throughout our lives [3, p. 106].

We can begin the exploration of our attitudes toward death by paying attention to the words we use when talking about it. Do we prefer euphemisms to direct language about death? If we want to reduce the possibility of being misunderstood, or of having what we say misinterpreted, direct language tends to be more helpful. Naturally, the language we use should be geared to the child's level of comprehension. This does not mean, however, substituting fantasy for facts or devising a sugar-coated version of the truth.

In addressing the second aspect of preparing ourselves to discuss death with children, we need not be anxious about becoming "experts" in the subject matter of death and dying. A healthy attitude toward death is not exclusively, or even necessarily, a result of specialized study. On the contrary, it goes hand-in-hand with a healthy attitude toward life, which naturally encompasses human experiences related to dying, death, and bereavement. Certainly, it can be useful to add to our knowledge of childhood developmental issues and to familiarize ourselves with the literature about children and death. As with any serious endeavor, knowledge increases our range of choices. Parents and other adults can obtain a wide range of resources from libraries and other community organizations [17-19].

UNDERSTANDING DEVELOPMENTAL ISSUES

Like other aspects of human development, children's understanding of death gradually evolves through the years of childhood and adolescence [20]. The interplay between experiences and the level of maturity that children bring to understanding them eventually leads to the possession of concepts and emotional responses that are substantially similar to those of adults in the children's culture [21]. Throughout the formative years, children's understanding of death tends to reflect a model of the world that is appropriate to their stage of development. However, when children experience death more directly, as when a parent or sibling dies, their understanding of death may change dramatically in a very brief period of time.

In the context of the assassination of President John F. Kennedy in 1963 and, more recently, with the explosion of the *Challenger* and the deaths of its crew, television kept millions of people informed about the course of events including the funeral ceremonies. In the process, a new social ritual was improvised: the television wake [22, p. xx]. With the death of the president, young children frequently expressed the fear that the assassin might be lurking in their neighborhood and they were concerned that something might happen to their parents, as it had to John-John's and Carolyn's father [22, pp. 222-223]. Teenagers expressed concern for the welfare of the president's family. They wondered about the political implications of the assassination, both domestically and internationally, particularly with respect to the Soviet Union, the United States' main adversary at the time [23]. The significance of the president's death was interpreted by young children and by adolescents in accordance with the concerns and issues that we would expect to prevail at their respective phases of development.

For young children, the central concern about death is likely to involve fears of separation from parents or other significant adults in their lives. Body image is also important, and young children express concerns about the integrity or mutilation of dead bodies. Fantasy reasoning, magical thinking, and realistic ideas about death may be conjoined in children's understanding of what makes people die and what "being dead" means. Typically, death is viewed as reversible, avoidable, or unnatural, being caused only by unusual events such as accidents or catastrophes. Many young children do not understand death as final or as something that could happen to them. This coincides with the Saturday morning cartoon version of death in which Daffy Duck is pressed to a thin sheet by a steamroller, only to pop up again a moment later as good as new—reversible death! Indeed, the understanding of death usually conveyed by the mass media is that it comes from outside, often violently, and that it is an accidental rather than natural process.

During the middle years of childhood, roughly ages six to eleven, children begin to think more logically about the objects and experiences in their lives. Their understanding of how people die reveals an ability to use concepts in a more concrete, logical fashion than is usually the case with younger children. They can name a wide range of causes of death, including disease, accidents, disasters, and old age.

As children grow through adolescence, their ability to think symbolically and engage in abstract reasoning advances further, resulting in sophisticated operations of thought that allow the prediction of complicated outcomes without having to try them out in the real world. By mentally manipulating related ideas and possibilities, the implications of an ethical or political issue can be hypothesized. Analysis and reflection are used to make sense of experience and to formulate a coherent model of the world. Death is understood as irreversible, final, universal, and inevitable, a biological fact that involves the cessation of physiological functioning.

GUIDELINES FOR DISCUSSING DEATH
WITH CHILDREN

In considering how to make the most of the teachable moments that arise in children's lives, the following guidelines deserve careful attention:

1. Be honest. Children of all ages have a right to expect honest responses to their questions. Adults should be willing to provide appropriate explanations in a straightforward and truthful manner.

2. Match the explanation to the child's ability to understand. This may mean acquiring further knowledge about how children develop cognitively and socially [3, 20, 24].

3. Supportive listening plays a crucial role. Paying attention to children's interests and questions provides a basis for responding to their particular circumstances and level of cognitive development.

4. Sensitive, caring communication is essential in all our interactions concerning death, dying, and bereavement [25]. We should remember, too, that we communicate nonverbally as well as verbally. When a child's pet dies and we rush out to get a replacement, that subtle "teaching" about death may have unintended consequences. Consider, for example, the case of a woman whose husband's death prompted her daughter to say, "Don't worry, Mommy, we'll get you another one."

5. When talking with children about death, verify with them what they think you have told them. Ask them what they have learned or understand about death from what you have said. In this way, the possibility of misunderstanding and confusion is minimized.

6. Do not put off introducing the topic of death to a child. When a comfortable pattern of communication about issues related to death has been established prior to the occurrence of a crisis, some of the confusion and uncertainty that would otherwise accompany painful trauma can be avoided.

EXPANDING OPPORTUNITIES
FOR LEARNING

The opportunities for discussing death with children and adolescents can be expanded by including death-related events that occur on a global scale. Issues involving war, famine, the plight of refugees and victims of disaster, along with other threats of violent death, are concerns for children as well as adults. Daniel Leviton, among others, has characterized such events as "horrendous deaths" [26]. Exposure to such tragedies cannot be prevented. They are brought to children's attention through accounts in the media as well as through social studies in school and the impromptu conversations of adults. Thus, even distant events become grist for the mill in children's developing perspectives on death and dying.

Although we may wish it were otherwise, efforts to protect youngsters from the disturbing news of death are ultimately futile. We need to engage their natural curiosity and use it as a guide for discussing tragic events in ways that cultivate appreciation of differing viewpoints and perspectives, as well as empathy for victims and survivors. Children who learn to talk openly about death and other crises are able to express their feelings and their need for social support [27]. This is a lesson that brings benefits throughout a lifetime. In discussing death with children through the ordinary experiences of life, we find that more than just cognitive or intellectual information is shared. Life is precious and precarious, yet that fact need not to make us fearful. In exploring with children how death is inextricably part of our lives, we discover that "teachable moments" can be nurturing moments as well.

REFERENCES

1. U. Carson, Teachable Moments Occasioned by "Small Deaths," in *Childhood and Death*, H. Wass and C. A. Corr (eds.), Hemisphere Publishing Corporation, Washington, D.C., 1984.
2. G. Rochlin, How Younger Children View Death and Themselves, in *Explaining Death to Children*, E. A. Grollman (ed.), Beacon Press, Boston, Massachusetts, 1967.
3. R. Kastenbaum, The Child's Understanding of Death: How Does It Develop?, in *Explaining Death to Children*, E. A. Grollman (ed.), Beacon Press, Boston, Massachusetts, 1967.
4. H. Wass and C. A. Corr, *Helping Children Cope with Death: Guidelines and Resources*, Hemisphere Publishing Corporation, Washington, D.C., 1982.
5. G. Stanford and A. E. Roark, Seizing the Teachable Moment: Social Learning in the Classroom, *People Watching, 2*:1, pp. 14-18, 1972.
6. N. M. McAloon, The Teachable Moment, *Journal of Reading, 36*:2, pp. 150-151, 1992.
7. M. Ryan, The Teachable Moment: The Washington Center Internship Program, *New Directions for Teaching and Learning, 35*, pp. 39-47, 1988.
8. R. E. Glasgow, et al., Changes in Smoking Associated with Hospitalization, *American Journal of Health Promotion, 6*:1, pp. 24-29, 1991.

9. L. Dubney, Working with the Elderly, *Journal of Applied Gerontology, 9*:1, pp. 118-128, 1990.
10. E. J. Tholen, *Home Energy Conservation Education*, paper presented at the Annual Meeting of the Illinois Sociological Association, 1981.
11. P. Fabiano, Peer-Based HIV Risk Assessment: A Step-by-Step Guide Through the Teachable Moment, *Journal of American College Health, 41*:6, pp. 297-299, 1993.
12. J. H. Salmela, Long-Term Intervention with the Canadian Men's Olympic Gymnastic Team, *Sport Psychologist, 3*:4, pp. 340-349, 1989.
13. C. A. Corr, C. M. Nabe, and D. M. Corr, *Death and Dying: Life and Living*, Brooks/Cole Publishing Company, Pacific Grove, California, 1993.
14. L. A. DeSpelder and N. Prettyman, *A Guidebook for Teaching Family Living*, Allyn and Bacon, Boston, Massachusetts, 1980.
15. E. Jackson, The Pastoral Counselor and the Child Encountering Death, in *Helping Children Cope with Death: Guidelines and Resources*, H. Wass and C. A. Corr (eds.), Hemisphere Publishing Corporation, Washington, D.C., 1982.
16. N. Reeves and D. Knowles, Helping Children Deal with Death Concerns, in *Death and Dying in the Classroom: Readings for Reference*, J. L. Thomas (ed.), Oryx Press, Phoenix, Arizona, 1984.
17. C. A. Corr, Books for Adults: An Annotated Bibliography, in *Helping Children Cope with Death: Guidelines and Resources*, H. Wass and C. A. Corr (eds.), Hemisphere Publishing Corporation, Washington, D.C., 1982.
18. H. Wass, Books for Children: An Annotated Bibliography, in *Helping Children Cope with Death: Guidelines and Resources*, H. Wass and C. A. Corr (eds.), Hemisphere Publishing Corporation, Washington, D.C., 1982.
19. J. L. Thomas, Materials for Children and Young Adults, in *Death and Dying in the Classroom: Readings for Reference*, J. L. Thomas (ed.), Oryx Press, Phoenix, Arizona, 1984.
20. L. A. DeSpelder and A. L. Strickland, Socialization: How We Learn About Death as Children, in *The Last Dance: Encountering Death and Dying* (3rd Edition), Mayfield Publishing Company, Mountain View, California, 1992.
21. M. W. Speece and S. B. Brent, The Acquisition of a Mature Understanding of Three Components of the Concept of Death, *Death Studies 16*:3, pp. 211-229, 1992.
22. M. Wolfenstein and G. Kliman (eds.), *Children and the Death of a President: Multi-Disciplinary Studies*, Anchor/Doubleday, Garden City, New York, 1966.
23. S. Ginsparg, A. Moriarty, and L. B. Murphy, Young Teen-Agers Responses to the Assassination of President Kennedy: Relation to Previous Life Experiences, in *Children and the Death of a President: Multi-Disciplinary Studies*, M. Wolfenstein and G. Kliman (eds.), Anchor/Doubleday, Garden City, New York, 1966.

24. H. Wass, Concepts of Death: A Developmental Perspective, *Childhood and Death*, H. Wass and C. A. Corr (eds.), Hemisphere Publishing Corporation, Washington, D.C., 1984.
25. A. L. Strickland and L. A. DeSpelder, Communicating about Death and Dying, in *A Challenge for Living: Dying, Death and Bereavement*, I. B. Corless, B. B. Germino, and M. Pittman (eds.), Jones and Bartlett, Boston, Massachusetts, 1995.
26. D. Leviton (ed.), *Horrendous Death, Health, and Well-Being*, Hemisphere Publishing Corporation, Washington, D.C., 1991.
27. S. Hetzel, V. Winn, and H. Tolstoshev, Loss and Change: New Directions in Death Education for Adolescents, *Journal of Adolescence, 14*, pp. 323-334, 1991.

CHAPTER 5

Perceptions of Death Through the Eyes of Children and Adolescents

Eleanor J. Deveau

> A child's life is like a piece of paper upon which each of us leaves a mark.
>
> — Chinese proverb

As professionals and parents, do we leave positive or negative "marks" when we respond to children's questions and concerns related to death? Though there is a greater tendency toward more open communication with children concerning death-related issues, many adults continue to be very uncomfortable with death as a topic for discussion [1]. Koocher maintains that we are still a "death-denying society" [2]. Many people believe that discussions about death threaten the innocence of childhood and, therefore, should be avoided.

Most parents prefer to keep death at a distance, protecting their children from the harsh reality of the pain and suffering that death engenders. Yet, most children think about death and need answers to their questions and concerns [1]. Left to their own devices, many children construct imaginative and elaborate explanations that are not grounded in reality. If they receive limited or misguided information, the "marks" that adults, parents, and professionals leave on their lives will have a negative influence on their understanding of death. Taken a step further, such negative marks may inhibit their ability to cope with the death of a close relative, friend, or pet; may delay their grief reactions; and may prevent them from completing the tasks of grieving [3].

In this chapter I will:

- provide a brief historical overview
- discuss the cognitive developmental approach as a foundation for most studies of children's conceptions of death, briefly exploring two relevant models
- examine the recent literature concerning four subconcepts which are associated with a mature understanding of death
- explore the content of children's art and provide a summary table outlining children's perceptions of death at different ages
- present some observations and considerations based on a pilot study of children's art.

BRIEF HISTORICAL OVERVIEW

Until the turn of the century, rural living in North America meant that death was an inherent part of life. Circumstances frequently exposed children to the death of farm animals, mothers dying during childbirth, siblings and peers dying of communicable diseases, and wakes in the home for deceased family members and neighbors. In the United States in 1900, over 50 percent of all deaths were children under fifteen years of age [4].

Historically, the gradual move to an urban society brought with it relocation of the sick and dying from their own homes to hospitals, the removal of the deceased from the family residence to funeral homes, and medical advances such as inoculations and improved sanitation that resulted in fewer deaths overall, especially deaths of children and infants.

As deaths declined and death was banished from the home, the hiding of death was characterized by a shift from cemeteries with tombstones to park or garden-like settings with names that dispelled any reference to the fact that dead people were buried there [5]. Even in children's books, references to dying and death virtually disappeared in the early 1900s and did not resurface until the 1970s [6].

As society shifted to an urban setting, families moved from life within the extended family to life in a nuclear family that was often remote from the influences and life experiences of grandparents and other relatives. In many households, death was acknowledged but often passed over with very little discussion. Children raised during this time of banishment, particularly those raised in an urban environment, frequently received little exposure and no grounding in dealing with death. When they became parents and were confronted with the death of a family member or friend, they had difficulty knowing how to cope themselves, let alone how to help their children. The absence of grandparents and extended family members who potentially had more life experiences, made the task even more difficult.

The pioneering research of Schilder and Wechsler [7], Anthony [8], Gesell and Hg [9], and Nagy [10] were the classic works of that time. It was not until the late 1950s and early 1960s that efforts to deal with understanding children's perceptions of death began to reappear in academic literature [11].

When public taboos on the delicate subjects of death and sexuality began to dissolve in the early 1970s, public figures such as Kübler-Ross used the media to enlighten society about dying and death. As part of the process, concerns about children's understanding of death began to be discussed in contemporary literature, public forums, and the media. Despite interest in this subject, the comfort level of parents and adults in discussing death with children and adolescents and helping them deal with the death of someone close has evolved slowly [12]. The belief that children should be shielded from the intense emotions accompanying death still prevails.

THE COGNITIVE DEVELOPMENTAL APPROACH

In our efforts as professionals to understand how death affects children, it is imperative to recognize that this understanding is frequently based on cognitive development and no matter what other variables are examined, cognitive development will always remain a key component [13].

Two models of the cognitive developmental approach will be examined in order to underpin an understanding of children's perceptions of death. The first, by Piaget, is a general model pertaining to four stages of child development [14, 15]. These are:

1. *The Sensorimotor Stage*—from birth to two years, is the time during which children think and feel through reflex activity. They manipulate objects and use their senses and movements in a trial and error approach to the world in which they are the center of attention.

2. *The Preoperative Stage*—from age two to seven years, involves children moving away from complete egocentricity. They begin to use language for thinking and learning, and use symbols to represent the external world. Through their cognitive processes, they gradually develop a representation of the concrete world.

However, the use of fantasy tends to flaw children's thinking, and their attempts at logic are incomplete.

3. *The Concrete Operations Stage*—from age seven to eleven years, is a time when children begin to be more logical and objective in their thinking. Their thoughts and actions are based on visible and concrete objects and events. They use a cause and effect approach that does not yet include abstract thought and reason.

4. *The Formal Operations Stage*—from age eleven years and beyond, incorporates the child's transition to adult thinking. Adolescents employ abstractions, theories, hypotheses, and logic in their understanding. They rely less on objects and events and are able to take a more in-depth approach to understanding and problem-solving.

Although Piaget's stages are frequently referred to by researchers, clinicians, and educators, the age ranges he suggests are less favored by those who are trying to understand children's perceptions of death. Piaget's model focuses on understanding the cognitive development of children in general rather than specifically addressing children's conceptions of death [11].

There have been many studies of children's understanding of death that are based on Piaget's stages but few have clearly articulated a detailed conceptual model that incorporates Piaget's work and includes age categories commonly used by today's professionals.

In the 1980s, the Lombardos developed an eclectic model which provides a potentially useful framework for outlining the stages of conceptions of death [16]. This includes:

1. *The Stage of Implied Misconceptions*—up to age two years, is a time when children have no accurate conception of death. This stage corresponds with Piaget's Sensorimotor Stage complete with egocentrism, manipulation of objects, and use of senses and movements in a trial and error approach to the world.

2. *The Stage of Gross Misconceptions*—from age two to five years, involves children's perception that death is gradual, temporary, and reversible. Children believe that life and body functions continue after death and they often compare death to sleeping or dreaming. Misconceptions arise from taking information literally and incorporating fantasy. Because of children's egocentrism, death is viewed as having someone taken away from them. For them, death is equated with separation and abandonment.

3. *The Stage of Refined Misconceptions*—from age five to nine years, relates to children's ability to begin to think in a cause and effect manner. There is a gradual transition toward logical thought and

they base their logic on real events. In this phase, death is viewed as "unnatural, irreversible, evitable, not universal, permanent, gradual and final" [16, p. 13]. This stage resembles Anthony's earlier work on the Stage of Erroneous Concepts [8].

4. *The Stage of Mature Conceptions*—beginning at nine years and extending into adolescence, involves the gradual conceptualization of death in abstract terms. During this stage death becomes inevitable, universal, and immediate. All bodily functions cease. These conceptual differences are indicative of changes toward abstract thought and problem-solving processes that are common in pre-adolescence and beyond.

The appeal of the Lombardos' approach is its practicality and potential for modification to include new information. Both Piaget and the Lombardos offer us the perspective that cognitive development is linear and progressive [11]. The majority of children by the age of eight are able to:

- group information and categorize it
- understand such groupings
- comprehend the status of an object and changes that may affect it
- develop a concept of time
- understand that others may think and feel differently than themselves
- problem-solve by working through a problem and back tracking to determine the steps involved
- learn from the experiences of others
- become less self-centered
- live up to societal standards and comply with rules and regulations
- increase their ability to be objective and insightful.

THE RESEARCH LITERATURE ON THE COGNITIVE DEVELOPMENTAL APPROACH

Prior to the 1980s, even though the cognitive developmental approach prevailed in the literature, difficulties arose concerning the reliability and validity of research studies based on cognition that addressed children's acquisition of a concept of death [1, 11, 17]. Problems were associated with the fact that:

- methodology varied as did the timing of when studies were conducted

- studies were cross-sectional as opposed to longitudinal
- specific variables such as socioeconomic level and religious background were not always controlled
- sample groups often were limited to the study of white middle-class children.

Nevertheless, in the early 1980s, Speece and Brent tried to compare and contrast age and developmental staging information from earlier studies which had identified a set of "several relatively distinct components" that form a mature concept of death [17, p. 211]. They concluded that three of these components or subconcepts[1] were useful in understanding children's perceptions of death. They are:

1. *Universality* (inevitability): refers to children's ability to conceptualize that death is universal and inevitable, including the reality that they too, will die.
2. *Irreversibility* (finality, irrevocability): refers to children's ability to conceptualize that dead people never come back to life.
3. *Nonfunctionality* (cessation, dysfunctionality): refers to children's ability to conceptualize that all biological, sensational, emotional, and cognitive functions have ceased [11].

Speece and Brent concluded that "a model age" for acquiring each subconcept is seven with approximately 60 percent of children achieving a mature understanding of all three concepts between the ages of five and seven years. They suggested that the requirement to be at least eight years old in order to understand these subconcepts, as suggested by some researchers, may be erroneous. They advocated the need to:

- understand the relationship between the "general" concept of child development as found in Piaget's model and each subconcept
- explore each subconcept in relation to the "other closely related" subconcepts including the need to examine the terms "alive," "inanimate," and "sick"
- determine the age at which children reach a "mature" understanding of each subconcept
- establish age consistency in future studies

---

[1] The terms universality, irreversibility, and nonfunctionality will be used in the remainder of this chapter. Alternate terms for these subconcepts, used by other authors, appear in brackets following each subconcept.

- explore the subconcepts in respect to plant and animal death as well as human death
- examine the impact of factors such as gender, religion, and experiences associated with death in the understanding of each subconcept [11].

In the same era as the work of Speece and Brent, Smilansky published her research based on a study of four to ten-year-old Israeli children [18]. She added a fourth concept, *causality*, to irreversibility, nonfunctionality, and universality. Causality is defined as children's ability to understand the objective causes of death—younger children tend to focus more on external causes while older children tend to focus more on internal causes [1, 18, 19].

In reviewing the literature, Smilansky found that all four subconcepts were understood earlier than anticipated. In contrast to studies in the United States which suggested that most children must be beyond age five and closer to ten years of age in order to understand nonfunctionality, Smilansky found that by the age of four years, Israeli children had no difficulty understanding nonfunctionality of sight, hearing, and motion. However, they did have some difficulty grasping concepts of cessation of feeling, thought, and consciousness. By age five, this difficulty was resolved for most of the children in her study [18].

A follow-up study, contrasting American children from lower socioeconomic levels with Smilansky's comparable group of Israeli children, revealed that Israeli children understood the subconcepts of irreversibility and nonfunctionality in advance of American children. Schonfeld and Smilansky suggested that the four subconcepts were learned longitudinally and progressively and that irreversibility, nonfunctionality, universality, and causality were learned in sequence [20]. Other studies from this era debated the sequencing and only agreed that causality was the last concept to be understood [1].

Since some studies suggested that there were differences in how children related the four subconcepts to people and animal deaths, Lazar and Torney-Purta, in their benchmark study published at the beginning of the 1990s, examined both of these factors in researching the four subconcepts. They analyzed two interview periods, spaced seven months apart, conducted with ninety-nine six and seven-year-old children [1]. Their findings included:

1. Children understood the subconcepts of irreversibility and universality first but there was no interdependence between these two subconcepts.

2. One of these two subconcepts must be understood before a child understood the subconcepts of either nonfunctionality or causality.
3. Irreversibility was understood by most children and changed little over seven months.
4. Universality was understood by the majority of the children by the end of the seven months.
5. The understanding of the subconcept of nonfunctionality, that is, the dead person's inability to hear, move, see, know, and feel, changed over the seven months so that 60 percent understood this concept in respect to animals and 47 percent in respect to humans.

Parents indicated that increases in their children's understanding at the end of the seven months were not related to any discussions that they may have had with them; children arrived at their own conclusions.

Lazar and Torney-Purta concluded that further studies should investigate the four subconcepts separately, in relation to one another, and over a period of time in order to understand the development of children's concepts of death.

Next, Speece and Brent re-examined the subconcepts of irreversibility, nonfunctionality, and universality in a study of ninety-one children between the ages of five years and nine months to ten years and two months [17]. Their subjects were enrolled in kindergarten through grade three, with each grade being represented equally and a girl/boy ratio of 5:4. Speece and Brent found that [17]:

• at least 50 percent of the children in each grade had a mature understanding of each individual subconcept,
• eighty percent of kindergarten children and almost all of the other children had a "mature understanding" of universality, with a smaller percentage achieving this at each grade level for the subconcepts of irreversibility and nonfunctionality,
• the number of children who understood irreversibility was greater than or equal to the number that understood nonfunctionality,
• irreversibility was more easily understood than nonfunctionality,
• the number of children who "achieved a mature understanding of irreversibility and nonfunctionality did not increase monotonically with age," i.e., more children in grade two demonstrated a mature understanding of these two subconcepts than did students in grade three. This finding may represent a common "transitional

regression" or a "stable change marking the advent of a more sophisticated and complex understanding of death" [17, p. 225],

- universality was understood before either irreversibility or nonfunctionality with the latter concepts being understood concurrently,
- the process of achieving a mature understanding of these three subconcepts continues for some children up to at least the age of ten years [17].

In recommending directions for further studies, Speece and Brent suggested:

- an extension of studies to incorporate both younger and older children,
- formal investigation of the components within each of the three subconcepts,
- replication of their study with populations of children from differing demographic backgrounds,
- examination of the effects of various death-related experiences on children's understanding of death [17].

These recommendations coincide with those of Lazar and Torney-Purta who highlight the need to examine children's answers to questions related to different referent objects. Their findings indicate a difference in the pattern of development of the subconcepts when the referent object is an animal as opposed to a person. They advocate the use of direct questioning to elicit information from children concerning how they think and feel about death [1].

In another interesting study, Speece and Brent examined the subconcept of irreversibility in a sample of 165 university undergraduates in order to contrast "the actual adult data to the presumed adult standard and to actual child data" [21]. They concluded that:

- many adults, like many of the older school-age children in their previous study, were less clear about irreversibility than younger children,
- adults, like these older children, had difficulty conceptualizing the boundary that marks the transition from life to death,
- irreversibility is a complex subconcept and is influenced by medical technology, the length of time a person is in a "death state," and clinical, ethical, and legal definitions of "alive and dead" [21, p. 24]. They state that:

Recent advances in medical knowledge and technology have interposed between the states of "unambiguously alive" and "unambiguously dead" and the new state, that of being "ambiguously alive," i.e., alive by virtue of the use of heroic life-support measures such as heart-and-lung machines and respirators [21, p. 27].

Conclusions From the Research

The following conclusions can be drawn from the above studies:

1. A framework that incorporates cognitive development and age is useful and necessary.
2. An updated definition of a mature adult concept of death is needed which takes into account advances in medical technology that continue to change the boundary between alive and dead [21].
3. Understanding the composition of the four subconcepts requires detailed study. Children may not grasp all aspects of a subconcept at the same time, that is, some aspects may be understood earlier than others.
4. Attainment of a "mature" understanding of the subconcepts probably occurs much earlier than previously anticipated for most children.
5. Questions concerning when the abstract thought processes of adulthood actually occur and how abstract thinking affects children's perceptions of death beyond the age of seven or eight years need to be addressed. For instance, is there a point in pre-adolescence or adolescence when children begin to reveal doubts similar to those exhibited by university students in Speece and Brent's study of irreversibility?
6. Culture, political turmoil, and hostile conflicts merit more attention. For example, the results of Nagy's research in the 1940s was likely influenced by war-time conditions in Hungary.

Clinicians and educators continue to struggle with how to integrate these research findings into their practice, especially when findings are inconclusive. They are challenged to find useful methods to determine what children are thinking and feeling about death at any given point in time. It is apparent that in any approach professionals should:

1. Pay close attention to the reality that children mature earlier than previously believed.
2. Consider the use of a cognitive developmental framework such as the one suggested by the Lombardos. This framework must be flexible in order to be useful.

3. Incorporate other mediums of expression, for example, children's drawings, to help understand and explain how they perceive death.

THE VALUE OF CHILDREN'S ART

Artwork is a medium through which children can spontaneously tell us what they think and feel in unfettered, uninhibited, and revealing illustrations [22]. Drawing provides them with the opportunity to express multiple feelings in a single image [23]. Children's drawings not only reveal their temporary or immediate feelings but may also reveal information about their personalities [24, p. 47].

Lonetto suggests that children's drawings:

- are a mixture of "motor and cognitive development"
- represent universal symbolic truths arising from their "unconscious views of the self in the world, or as representations of learned cultural symbols"
- are subjective perceptions of their world
- often represent what they know and understand rather than what they see
- tend to show increasing object differentiation with age
- are "symbolic, perceptual measures of expected interactions with the world" which can be used "as a way of combining, testing, and changing related concepts" [24, p. 48]
- may be complex and contain much that is of psychological value [24].

In his study, Lonetto asked children what happened when people died, did they think about death, did everyone die, and did they think they would die some day. His sample included 201 Canadian children ages three years and five months through to thirteen years. The results of his study of their artwork are summarized in the following section.

CHILDREN'S PERCEPTIONS OF DEATH: FACTORS INVOLVED AND CONTENT OF THEIR ARTWORK

The following review of the four subconcepts of death and related anxieties is based on the author's experiences and the findings from related literature and research. Brief but relevant information is provided using common age ranges and includes condensed findings from Lonetto's extensive study of children's drawings [24].

CHILDREN UP TO SIX YEARS OF AGE

Universality

Young children, especially under the age of three years, exempt themselves from the possibility of death. However, if someone close to them dies, they may believe that someone else may also die.

Irreversibility

This age group believes that death is reversible and that the dead live on somewhere else such as in the cemetery. Death is often associated with sleep. Lonetto cites the case of one child who drew a picture of a dead person lying down. The child said that in order to make the dead person come to life, you simply had to turn the page around [24].

Nonfunctionality

Children in this age range believe that the dead see, talk, eat, and walk around. One three-year-old girl wanted to know where Grandpa's ladder was so that he could climb out of his coffin, do his shopping, and find someone to do his cooking.

Causality

For young children, death may be associated with being good or bad, that is, they believe what happens is a result of how they behave. Death is also linked to darkness or fantasy. Because children think in concrete terms, they may connect death to killing themes in which people die from accidents or violent acts. Possible causes of death in this age range include old age, monsters, the consequences of bad acts, doctors, hospitals, and separation (i.e., kidnapping and hiding) [24].

Anxieties

The predominant fear for these young children is the fear of being separated from their parents, especially their mother. This anxiety may be intense and surface when children believe that they will be left alone. There is a strong association between being dead and being left alone. Because magic and fantasy are often intertwined with children's thinking, other fears may be present, such as the fear that if you pull the plug in the bathtub you might go down the drain.

Lonetto's study of children's drawings in this age range reflected the following:

- one color was used most often: boys preferred black and girls used red or purple
- bodies were "amoeboid" with "stick-like appendages"
- age and sex were usually undetermined but some figures had male traits
- bodies were usually standing or lying down
- faces were drawn smiling [24].

CHILDREN SIX THROUGH EIGHT YEARS OF AGE

The literature becomes more controversial with respect to what actually transpires in this age range.

Universality

Children begin to recognize that people who they previously believed were exempt from death will die, probably including themselves. Some children know that death signifies the end of life on earth. Uncertainty still exists as to whether all children see death as inevitable by the end of this phase [24].

Irreversibility

It is suggested that in this age range children move toward understanding that death is irreversible. Death can mean the end of life as they know it. However, the work of Speece and Brent raises the possibility that advances in medical technology may interfere with this perception [21].

Nonfunctionality

Children recognize that the dead do not move, see, talk, breathe, or eat. They may also acknowledge that hearing, smelling, and all other bodily functions cease completely.

Causality

Some researchers suggest that children in this age group externalize death and personify it as a monster, ghost, or skeleton who can "rob you of your life," **but** if you see it coming you can escape or avoid its grasp [10; 24, p. 92]. Other causes of death include old age (though sometimes the death of a child is acknowledged), illness, accidents, and killings.

Anxieties

The main fear of children in this age range has shifted from fear of separation from parents to fear of bodily injury or mutilation. Death is viewed as scary, frightening, disturbing, and dangerous. Children become concerned about the ceremonies and rituals associated with the dead [24].

In Lonetto's study, he found that drawings included the following:

- caskets, crosses, and tombstones
- life symbols such as the sky, sun, clouds, flowers, and trees
- figures which were drawn walking, standing, or lying in caskets or beds
- figures usually of undetermined age
- most faces drawn smiling, but occasionally the mouth was drawn frowning or in pain [24].

CHILDREN AGES NINE THROUGH TWELVE YEARS

Though this period is viewed as a bridge between childhood and adolescence, its importance has been downplayed or overlooked in child development [24]. Yet, it is in this period that children move through many changes in how they think, feel, and act, and eventually achieve the ability to reason, think abstractly, and problem-solve like adults. Their poetry, stories, and art reflect their movement toward abstract thought. Pre-adolescence has been recognized by some authorities as a time when the harsh realities of the world truly sink in. Although children are still largely controlled by adults, their quest for independence begins. They want to be individuals with rights and privileges, but they still carry the mantle of childhood.

Universality

The acknowledgment that everyone dies, including themselves, appears to be understood by the beginning of this age range or earlier.

Irreversibility

In the past, it was accepted that children in this age group believed that death was definitely irreversible. However, advances in medical technology including resuscitation and organ transplants, pose questions regarding the boundaries between life and death and may create uncertainties regarding this subconcept.

Nonfunctionality

Most children by the beginning of this age range recognize that all bodily functions cease completely when someone dies.

Causality

Children realize that death occurs as a result of the deterioration of the body as well as a full range of internal and external causes including illness, disease, shootings, stabbings, accidents, disasters, war, and suicide. They are concerned about the relationship between illness and death. Most younger children in this age group believe that old age is the cause of many deaths. They gradually include deaths of children and young people, but continue to believe that death is still far away in the future.

Anxieties

Children express interest in and concern about the rituals of burial and have various anxious feelings in relation to what will happen when and after they die. These include how much they will suffer, where their bodies will go after death (heaven or hell), whether they will suffocate, whether their bodies will deteriorate, and how death will impact on them and their families. The ability to use abstract thought may amplify these concerns as illustrated by the question of one eleven-year-old boy who asked, "What happens to the person as a human being when he dies . . . does he **just** cease to exist?"

Because each age within this group of children has some unique characteristics, Lonetto divided his findings concerning their drawings accordingly:

Art at Nine Years Reflected

- concern over the death of particular people, especially grandparents
- burial rites and practices
- death related to old age, illness, and disease
- some smiling faces but sad faces were now drawn
- some deaths as bad and others as full of fear

- life symbols such as sky, grass, sun, and flowers, with the exception of water [24].

Art at Ten Years Indicated

- death as horrible, terrible, and frightening
- the place of death as full of "darkness and gloom"
- less concern about burial rites
- less concern about the ways in which people died except for murder or painful death
- death could occur at any age, but for the first time the death of a mother was acknowledged by some [24].

Art at Eleven Years Revealed

- fear of being buried alive
- concerns about being eaten by worms or bugs even though the body was in a casket; some children recognized that they would avoid being eaten if they were cremated
- dying should be painless and when people died they should not suffer [24].

Art at Age Twelve Years Showed

- death as "profound darkness or blackness"
- boys depicted death as "horrible, terrible, scary, or painful"
- girls saw death as scary but also heartbreaking, especially in relation to burial
- almost one half did not draw human figures, some drew abstract forms
- drawing of life symbols included water
- burial symbols such as "tombstones, caskets, and wreaths" which were often abstract in form
- human figures as sombre, "slightly evil," or sad
- no smiling faces but rather faces drawn with frowns, sneers, or a look of fear
- the dead usually of undetermined age
- few acts of death by external agents [24].

In summary, for children from nine through twelve years of age, Lonetto described the following common concerns in their drawings: awareness of self-mortality; distinct fears of death; interest in rituals of death; and feelings about the inevitability of death [24]. The transition from drawing happy faces to sad faces provides evidence to support these concerns and signifies the loss of childhood innocence concerning death.

ADOLESCENCE

Adolescents' Perspectives on Death[2]

Adolescents have distinct concerns and capabilities in relation to dying and death that have a separate focus from those of younger children. The early adolescent becomes aware of the personal and family implications of death, whereas the older adolescent attempts to impart meaning to death as well as to life [12]. There is considerable transition in thought and understanding during these years [25].

We know that adolescents are deluged with change. They are neither children nor adults but young people who are passing through a phase of life filled with rapid physical growth, sexual maturation, and specific cognitive and emotional needs [26]. The literature has characteristically portrayed adolescence as a time of disruption, turmoil, and rebellion [12]. Adolescence is also a time of transitions, and teens often vacillate as they struggle with their parents and society's expectations of them. Through all this, they strive for independence and the freedom to make their own choices and decisions [25].

Although commonly viewed as a single phase of life, adolescence consists of three distinct phases [25].

Early Adolescence: The young adolescent is capable of logical thought, tends to be dependent on parents, and is easily influenced. Role modeling is accepted; parents are still friends and sometimes even companions. These teens are more compliant to demands and more willing to work within the boundaries of parental structure. They may do some experimenting which is influenced by culture and peers. Anxieties tend to focus on physical and sexual changes and peer relationships [27].

Middle Adolescence: This phase which coincides with age sixteen, is usually the peak of turmoil and rebellion. These teens are prone to emotional fluctuations and extreme reactions. They often exhibit a fight-or-flight response: girls typically shout and slam doors, while boys may isolate themselves in their rooms [28]. Middle adolescents become judgmental, try to bargain with adults, and feel that they "know it all." Parents may become their "worst enemies," peers become a priority,

[2] This section on adolescence includes excerpts from the author's article, *The Impact on Adolescents when a Sibling is Dying* [25].

and they often experiment or break rules as they try to establish their own beliefs and values. As they seek their independence, they struggle with dependency needs, sexuality issues, and their own self-images [29].

Late Adolescence: The rationality and increasing maturity of older adolescents allow them to function with less denial and overt emotion than their younger counterparts. They complete their physical and sexual maturation, clarify their ethics and values, and continue to acquire adult social skills. They begin to move into new social spheres and try to find peers and perhaps a mate with similar values. As they continue to establish their own independence, they may separate from their family of origin and begin to make long-term commitments, including career decisions [12, 27].

Though there are many changes attributed to adolescence, there does not appear to be a clear understanding of how adolescent perceptions of death are reflected in their artwork. In addition, it is more difficult to review perceptions of death in the same manner as for younger children because the four subconcepts of universality, irreversibility, nonfunctionality, and causality are expected or assumed to be part of their repertoire. However, there are some issues that merit attention under each of these subconcepts.

Universality

When adolescents take physical risks, Gordon suggests that even though they may not realize that they are "flirting with death" their behavior is "counterphobic" and involves a "challenge to death wherein each survival of risk is a victory over death." She continues: "High risk activities are ways of testing the body while still remaining cloaked in the remnants of belief in immortality" [12, p. 27]. Perhaps adolescents who engage in risk-taking behavior are challenging the universality of death thus defying the reality that they will die if they tempt fate.

Irreversibility

As previously mentioned, there is a point in pre-adolescence or adolescence when teens begin to doubt that death is irreversible. This appears to be closely linked to abstract thought and reasoning. Doubts concerning irreversibility may be fueled by: a) the advances in medical technology (e.g., cardiac resuscitation and organ transplants) that reverse fatal conditions thus halting the dying process; b) accounts of life after death experiences; c) advances in genetic engineering which can create or alter life; d) legal and ethical debates concerning the status of being alive or dead [21]; and e) the study of cryogenics that may offer the potential to freeze bodies for rejuvenation in future years.

Such realities, discussions, and possibilities may enhance some adolescents' beliefs that anything is possible.

The increasing rate of suicide among adolescents may imply that they do not contemplate the full consequences of this act. Gordon suggests that suicide may indicate that teens deny the physical results and finality of such a death [12].

Nonfunctionality

If some adolescents have doubts about the subconcept of irreversibility, they may also question nonfunctionality. Medical technology which can maintain the body in a "life-like state" on life-support systems challenges the status of being alive or dead and creates doubts about the cessation of bodily functions. For example, when one teen suffered a fatal brain injury in a car accident, his friends had difficulty distinguishing between "dead" and "brain dead." They did not understand how parts of the body could be maintained in a living state while the "brain waves" were flat, indicating that their friend was technically dead.

Causality

Once irreversibility and nonfunctionality are questioned, some adolescents may also doubt certain accepted internal and external causes of death. Given the numerous advances in medical technology, conditions exist that are no longer fatal. The belief that these medical advances will continue to expand and include other diseases and afflictions may instill more doubts and further challenge all four subconcepts.

Anxieties

When adolescents daydream they frequently reflect upon both past and present concerns. The imagination that is woven into these daydreams is similar to that of younger children but magical thinking is not usually present. Daydreaming may provide relief from thoughts about death, especially their own death. On the other hand, some daydreams may harbor anxieties that accentuate their concerns and fears as illustrated in this question posed by Mark, a thirteen-year-old: "When you die and you are looking down at yourself . . . can you call out to everyone you know to save you from dying?"

For other adolescents, anxiety may surface when they feel compromised or overwhelmed. Such anxieties may be associated with failure at school, loss of social support, injury, or serious illness. The death of a close relative or friend may threaten their personal integrity and well-being as well as generate fears associated with existential concerns about life beyond death. After the death of his uncle, John, fourteen years old, struggled with recurrent episodes of panic because he could not sort out what happens to the soul after death. He questioned: "Is that **all** there is, you live . . . then you die, and then there is **nothing**? How do you know what's on the other side? . . . What if it's just nothingness, darkness . . . ?"

Other emotions surface when adolescents think about death. Maurer, in her studies during the early 1960s, found that statements about death made by teens seventeen to nineteen years of age were replete with references to sadness, loneliness, and uncertainty. Some adolescents described death as peaceful and beautiful but also expressed a distaste for dead people and the smells associated with funerals [30]. Some references in relation to personification about death paralleled similar concerns of children between the ages of nine to twelve years.

If we consider the ages of nine to twelve years as a time of "benign latency" [31], then late adolescence can be regarded as a time of possible "benign adolescence"—a period which is less burdened by the emotional intensity evident in the other two adolescent phases. Perhaps to do so would be reasonable given the fact that this period portrays more stability. However, such a distinction may underestimate or not adequately reflect the depth of cognition, emotion, understanding, and growing maturity characteristic of these teens. We can expect late adolescents to grasp both the realities and abstractions of death in a more comprehensive manner than younger adolescents and children. The depth of such comprehension will be clearly illustrated in the description of a drawing by Julie, age seventeen years, in the next section of this chapter.

In an attempt to summarize children and adolescents' understanding of death at different ages from the above findings in the literature and research studies, Table 1 provides an overview of the four subconcepts of universality, irreversibility, nonfunctionality, and causality in relation to the common age ranges for children. For each age range, this table also includes usual anxieties and condensed findings from Lonetto's studies of children's artwork.

PILOT PROJECT

Drawing provides a simple, straightforward technique or medium through which children and adolescents can express their thoughts and feelings without the use of language. A small pilot project was initiated

Table 1. Children and Adolescents' Understanding of the Subconcepts of Death at Different Ages

	Up to 6 Years	6 through 8 Years	9 through 12 Years	Adolescence
Universality	No	Possible → probable	Yes	Yes but may challenge
Irreversibility	No	Partial → probable or yes	Yes but uncertain	Yes but may question
Nonfunctionality	No	Some → all functions	Yes	Yes but may question
Causality	External forces good vs. bad	External forces and some internal	Full range both internal and external	Yes but may question
Anxieties/fears	Separation anxiety	Mutilation anxiety Death = scary, frightening, dangerous Concern over ceremonies and rituals associated with death	Suffocation anxiety Fear of suffering Concern over deterioration of body, burial rituals, impact of death on family, and heaven and hell Dying should be painless, without suffering Girls: death = scary, heartbreaking Boys: death = horrible, scary, painful	Fear of suffering Fear of painful death Fear of the unknown after death
Features in artwork	Stick-like figures Body standing or lying Undetermined age and gender ☺	Death = monster Caskets, crosses and tombstones Life symbols ☺	Life symbols → symbol of water at age 12 included Death = bad, fearful → horrible, terrible Full of darkness and gloom, blackness Burial symbols → more abstraction Some human figures → abstract forms Sombre or evil figures Color black used most by boys and girls ☺ → ☹	More abstract forms and figures Fewer humans drawn More symbols of death Tears, sadness ☹
Causes of death	Old age, accidents, killings, monsters, bad acts, doctors, hospitals, separation (kidnapping, hiding)	Monster to be avoided, accidents, killings	Deterioration of body, shootings, stabbings, accidents, illness, disease, natural disasters, war, suicide	Accidents, suicide, natural disasters, war, illness, disease
How old are people when they die?	Old	Old, occasionally child dies	Old → young → any age	Any age

which involved children from five to seventeen years of age in an effort to determine: 1) if children who have had no personal death-related experiences still think about death, conceptualize issues related to death, and readily portray this understanding through their artwork; and 2) if their artwork is in keeping with the literature and the findings from Lonetto.

Data Collection

The children and adolescents in this project were middle-class Canadians who had not experienced the death of someone close to them. They were Protestant, Roman Catholic, or from families where no particular faith was practiced. Each child and adolescent was healthy and free of any acute or chronic illness, had no physical limitations, and was enrolled in an age-appropriate grade at school. The population selected was very restricted primarily because these children were most accessible and their parents were willing to permit their involvement.

Each child was asked to draw a picture of what happens when people die or what death means to them. They were given an uncolored piece of paper and could use any colors from the numerous crayons and pencils that were provided.

Based on the recommendations of other researchers who suggest direct questioning to elicit useful information [1], children were asked the following questions in addition to the request for an explanation of their pictures: 1) What happens to people after they die? and 2) How do people die? Some children were probed for other information when further clarification was required of their explanations or drawings.

Findings

The following pages contain a sampling of the drawings. Each drawing is followed by the child or adolescent's personal account of his or her picture and the responses to the questions that were asked.

Michael, Five Years Old

Tell me about your picture:

When you die you go into the graveyard. I know who the graveyard is—its God's. Here's the church and somebody died. There's bows for decorations when somebody dies. God's in the cloud.

What happens to people after they die?

> When people die we dig a hole down below and God pulls them up
> and then God uses a machine that turns them into an angel—or I
> guess he has powers that turn them into an angel.

How do people die?

> um . . . when they eat bad food, the bad food sticks to their heart
> and the blood can't get in the heart and then you have a heart
> attack . . . or something like that.

Karl, Seven Years Old

Tell me about your picture:

> An angel has come down from heaven to see how many people were
> dead and take them up to heaven. Coffins are buried in the ground
> and there are stones on top with the people's names. A live person
> is giving flowers to one of the stones. A bird is flying in the sky but
> he can't see the angel.

What happens to people after they die?

In heaven they turn into angels. But, if they were bad then the devil will take them back to the ground and they will turn into something else.

How do people die?

Somebody kills them, they get run over by a car, they have a heart attack or something like that.

Jason, Nine Years Old

Jason's explanation:

Two men relatives are lowering the coffin. They are crying because they are sad. The priest is saying all the stuff that you say at the cemetery. God is up in heaven lifting his hands because he's bringing somebody into his kingdom.

What happens to people after they die?

> . . . bodies rise to the kingdom of God or they go to the devil.

How do people die?

> . . . murder, heart attack, suicide, cancer, or asthma.

Why did you use the color purple?

> . . . because it's one of the colors of death.

Paul, Ten Years Old

His explanation:

> This is a funeral home where people go before they get buried and where people go to pray. The coffin is brown and the top is open so you can see the person that died for the last time.

What happens to people after they die?

The body gets taken to the funeral home and after a while it gets buried. It decays and becomes part of the ground. The soul usually goes to heaven, I think . . . right away if the person has no sins. If he's got sins when he dies the soul goes to purgatory for his sins to be forgiven by God. If he has too many sins then he goes to hell. But this dead person's soul went to heaven.

How do people die?

. . . heart attack, cancer, high cholesterol, old age, they get shot or murdered.

Patrick, Eleven Years Old

Patrick's explanation:

A person has died of natural causes because he was really old. As he died, his spirit moved out of his body toward a bright light. His spirit is peaceful and goes towards the light because it wants to be in heaven with God.

How do other people die?

. . . sometimes young kids die of cancer and cystic fibrosis, earthquakes, tornadoes, floods, reckless shootings, drunk driving too.

Greg, Twelve Years Old

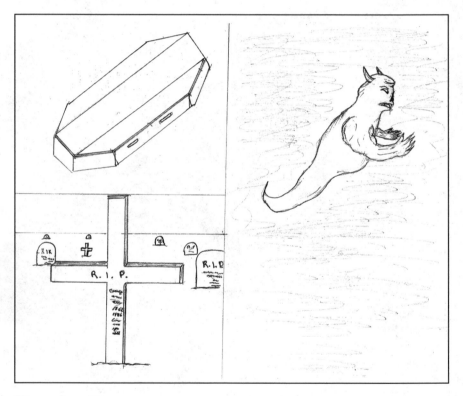

His explanation:

In the top left corner the coffin is a symbol of death. In the bottom left corner the graveyard is a symbol but also a place where people go after they die. On the right is what death looks like to me . . . it's a spirit . . . it has horns, a nose and is vicious because it will come along and rob you of your life. After a person dies their spirit goes either to heaven or to hell . . . it depends on what kind of person they were.

What happens after people die?

The body gets buried, it lies there unused as the spirit is gone. It lies there and rots.

How do people die?

Accidents, suicide, natural death from old age, part of their body ceases to work or they develop diseases. Wars should also be included.

Karen, Thirteen Years Old

Tell me about your picture:

> This is a picture of a family. The dad has just died and is lying in a coffin. They all miss him because he was very young.

What happens after people die?

> They're buried . . . I don't know.

How do people die?

> they're sick sometimes . . . I guess, I don't know . . .

Tim, Fifteen Years Old

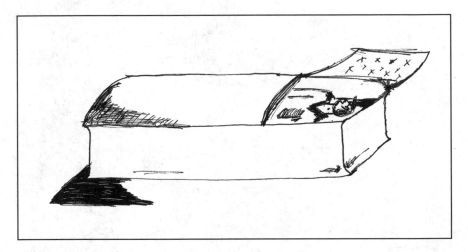

Tim's explanation:

> This is a coffin with probably a male person inside.

What happens after people die?

> I'm not really sure. People are sad because the person is not around any more. I guess the person goes to heaven . . . but this is probably open to discussion!

How do people die?

> suicide, drunk driving, accidents, things like that . . . sometimes they're very sick or have a terrible disease.

Julie, Seventeen Years Old

Julie's explanation:

> The person who is dead is lying in the coffin. The body is there but there is nothing inside—that's why there's no face. It's lifeless like a sleep. The body is like an empty container. The stuff that was inside—the soul—has gone to heaven.

How do people die?

> It's God's wish . . . it's destiny and fate.

Why did you use the colors black and red?

> The black symbolizes emptiness—the absence of everything else. The red is the background and represents the memory and love of the people that live on and remember the person that has died.

DATA ANALYSIS AND DISCUSSION

Descriptions of each child and adolescent's drawing were recorded. Operating on the premise that children are the best authorities to explain their artwork, a discussion of the findings is presented, however, no in-depth analysis was attempted because of "the danger of reading into another's creation . . ." "Each drawing is a unique creation, reflecting the one who drew it. The image may appear to be one thing to the viewer, yet is something quite different to its creator . . ." [32, p. 17].

The following discussion of each child and adolescent's drawing helps us to appreciate the need to take the time to listen and let them describe their drawings in detail. Perhaps we should be less concerned about where a particular child fits into the developmental continuum and more concerned with what thoughts, feelings, and anxieties he or she is sharing with us.

Michael at the age of five years is concerned with burial, fantasy, and the world beyond. He integrates modern technology into his account of how God converts the dead into angels after hauling them up to heaven. His description of how people die is very concrete and practical, in keeping with what might be expected at his age.

Karl, age seven, portrays a great interest in the image of angels as invisible beings who remove the deceased and take them to heaven. He draws happy faces and incorporates life symbols into a scenario linked to the concrete setting of the graveyard. In keeping with his cause and effect reasoning he explains that the devil will take care of those who do bad things.

Jason, at nine years, illustrates the sadness and tears of the relatives of the deceased. He combines the concrete rituals of burial carried out at the cemetery by the relatives and the priest with the mystical worlds of heaven and hell. His list of causes of death include self-inflicted deaths, in addition to those resulting from illness and violent acts.

Paul, ten years old, draws a detailed scene in a funeral home, and then moves on to describe his perception of what happens to the body and soul after death. He believes that the body decays. He identifies moral acts as the final determinant for the eventual destination of the "soul." Paul lists both violent and medical causes of death and mentions modern-day concerns of the dangers of high cholesterol.

Patrick, at eleven years, provides a thought-provoking image of what he believes happens after a person dies. His description of an after-death experience has the dimension of peace and the movement of the spirit. The spirit is the abstract component of the soul which moves toward the light, an abstract symbol of God. In earlier research, it was assumed that this degree of abstraction was reserved for children twelve years of age and beyond. Patrick's list of causes of death includes deaths of children from serious diseases and those resulting from natural disasters.

Greg, twelve years old, defines death in abstract terms as a vicious spirit that is horrible and frightening. He only uses the color black and incorporates the imagery of the graveyard in keeping with Lonetto's findings. He recognizes that the spirit is gone after death leaving behind only rotting remains. Greg adds wars to the list of causes of death reflecting a more complete range of possibilities.

Karen, at thirteen years of age, reflects an intense anxiety and sadness about death, especially the death of someone close. She was unable to talk about her thoughts and feelings any further.

Tim, fifteen years old, suggests that death involves sadness and uncertainty. His explanation alludes to the debate about what actually happens after someone dies. He adds drunk driving to the list of causes of death and includes those resulting from disease and accidents.

Julie, at age seventeen, produces a deceptively simple drawing which reflects a depth of insight that far exceeds the thoughts of the younger adolescents and children. Her description is steeped in abstraction linking colors, feelings, and the soul with the concrete reality of the body and the survivors that are left behind. In keeping with her beliefs, death is a result of destiny and fate.

SUMMARY

At times, the variety of descriptions and responses from the children and adolescents contributed to some difficulty in delineating if all of them were age-appropriate and incorporated what was expected from the literature and existing studies. Although this was a small pilot project with many limitations as previously noted, the drawings did support: a) much of the existing literature, b) Lonetto's findings, c) the fact that children readily portray their understanding of death and death-related issues through their artwork, and d) children who have not experienced the death of a close relative, friend, or pet still think about death and what it means to them [1].

Considerations for Further Research

Further research should involve children and adolescents from different socioeconomic, cultural, ethnic, and religious backgrounds in a carefully structured study comparable to Lonetto's earlier work. Other variables that deserve more attention include:

1. Family—How do communication and interaction patterns, family composition, roles of family members, and socioeconomic status influence children's perceptions? How does domestic violence impact on children's fears and anxieties related to death?
2. Culture and ethnic background—What role does culture and ethnicity play? For instance, the imposition of Christianity on Native American children and their families coupled with the suppression of their cultural and ethnic beliefs, values, and practices have had a serious impact on how these children perceive and understand death-related issues.
3. Religion—To what extent do religious beliefs and practices influence how children think and feel about death? Do these beliefs instill fear or comfort?
4. Rituals and customs—How do rituals and practices associated with burial rites help children develop a better understanding of death? Do differences in burial practices influence children's perceptions of death? For instance, in some geographical locations the method of burial is controlled by climate and terrain, such as in Newfoundland and New Orleans where bodies must be buried above ground.
5. Children exposed to life-threatening illnesses—Studies indicate that seriously ill children and those who are dying have an accelerated or advanced understanding of death [33, 34]. How

      do children living with a parent or sibling who is dying perceive death differently?

6. Nature of the death—How does a sudden death by accident, suicide, or homicide affect children's perceptions of death and reactions to grief?

7. Age of the person who died—How does the death of a peer or sibling influence anxieties and perceptions concerning death?

8. Gender differences—How do gender differences affect children's perceptions, attitudes, and reactions concerning death? How and why do these differences evolve?

9. The media—What is the long-term impact on children and adolescents' perceptions of death when they frequently view television programs filled with repeated episodes of violence, murder, and suicide [35]? Does this exposure desensitize them to the reality and meaning of death? How does the sensationalism of murder and suicide by the media influence children and adolescents' thinking regarding these matters?

10. Political conflict and war—How are children's attitudes and perceptions of death affected and/or changed by their exposure to devastating military destruction in war-torn areas such as Sarajevo? Do they reach a more mature level of understanding at an earlier age as may be implied by the work of Smilansky [18]?

A FINAL NOTE ON CHILDREN AND ADOLESCENTS' PERCEPTIONS OF DEATH

Though there is a growing body of literature concerning death awareness in children and adolescents, much remains to be learned [32, p. 20]. Perhaps much of this learning should be through the eyes of children—through their artwork, poems, and stories which provide unique insights into their world and their understanding of the role that death plays in that world.

Research has yielded useful, thought-provoking information. However, a major difficulty lies in how to interpret what has transpired through the more than five decades since the first relevant research was published. For example, we recognize that there is a need to be flexible in our expectations and interpretations of what children say and draw. It is likely that North American children reach a mature understanding of the subconcepts of universality, irreversibility, nonfunctionality, and causality earlier in their development than previously believed. Although their understanding has the potential of being sequential or linear, there is no guarantee that perceptions of death will develop in such a manner.

What previously had been acknowledged as distinct stages of development appear to be phases which involve a certain amount of fluidity or vacillation between the years and the levels of understanding. There do not appear to be any absolutes. By the same token, children's understanding of the subconcepts of death is less permanent than previously thought. For instance, adolescence may be a stage in which perceptions of death are contemplated, unraveled, and reconstructed into a different format. Later, in early adulthood, a similar process may occur with at least the subconcept of irreversibility being open to question, perhaps indefinitely [11].

As children and adolescents question issues related to death and vacillate in their understanding concerning such matters, external forces in today's society add a new dimension to their deliberations. Do major advancements in medical technology have such an impact that children receive a message which suggests "Gone today, but here tomorrow?" Perhaps the inevitability of one's own death is less believable given the medical advances that halt or reverse the dying process? How do ethical and legal debates concerning the ability to create life, alter life, prolong life, prevent life, and terminate life through genetic engineering, organ transplants, abortion, and euthanasia affect children and adolescents' ability to reach any understanding about issues related to either life or death? Does repeated exposure to violence and death in the media desensitize children to the reality of death and promote less respect for life?

A plethora of external forces impact upon children and adolescents and likely contribute to confusion concerning their perceptions of death. These forces will continue to multiply over time. Our challenge as professionals and parents is to temper the impact of the external forces that leave negative "marks" on children and adolescents' lives and profoundly affect their self-concepts and perceptions concerning both life and death. Our other challenge is to be available to children and adolescents as they ponder life and death-related issues. The positive "marks" that we leave on their lives are directly influenced by our understanding, knowledge, patience, and, most of all, our honesty.

REFERENCES

1. A. Lazar and J. Torney-Purta, The Development of the Subconcepts of Death in Young Children: A Short Term Longitudinal Study, *Child Development, 62*, pp. 1321-1333, 1991.

2. G. Koocher, *Coping with the Death of a Child: Preventive Interventions*, plenary session, Children's Hospice International Conference Sydney, Australia, June 1993.

3. S. Fox, Helping Child Deal with Death Teaches Valuable Skills, *The Psychiatric Times*, pp. 10-11, August 1988.

4. D. Fredlund, The Remaining Child, in *Home Care for the Dying Child: Professional and Family Perspectives*, I. M. Martinson (ed.), Appleton-Century-Crofts, New York, 1976.

5. P. Ariès, *Western Attitudes Toward Death from the Middle Ages to the Present*, The John Hopkins University Press, Baltimore, 1974.

6. J. G. Marshall and V. W. Marshall, The Treatment of Death in Children's Books, *Omega, 2*, pp. 36-44, 1971.

7. P. Schilder and D. Wechsler, The Attitude of Children Towards Death, *Journal of Genetic Psychology, 45*, pp. 406-451, 1934.

8. S. Anthony, A Study of the Development of the Concept of Death, *British Journal of Educational Psychology, 9*, pp. 276-277, 1939.

9. A. Gesell and F. L. Hg, *The Child from Five to Ten*, Harper and Brothers, New York, 1946.

10. M. Nagy, The Child's Theories Concerning Death, *Journal of Genetic Psychology, 73*, pp. 3-27, 1948.

11. M. W. Speece and S. B. Brent, Children's Understanding of Death: Three Components of a Death Concept, *Child Development, 55*, pp. 1671-1685, 1984.

12. A. K. Gordon, The Tattered Cloak of Immortality, in *Adolescence and Death*, C. A. Corr and J. N. McNeil (eds.), Springer Publishing Company, New York, 1986.

13. R. Kastenbaum, The Child's Understanding of Death: How Does it Develop?, in *Explaining Death to Children*, E. A. Gröllman (ed.), Beacon Press, Boston, 1967.

14. J. Piaget, *The Science of Education of the Psychology of the Child*, Grossman, New York, 1970.

15. J. Piaget, *The Language and Thought of the Child*, Routledge Kegan Paul, London, 1959.

16. V. S. Lombardo and E. F. Lombardo, Kids Grieve Too, Charles C. Thomas Publishers, Springfield, Illinois, 1986.

17. M. W. Speece and S. B. Brent, The Acquisition of a Mature Understanding of Three Components of the Concept of Death, *Death Studies, 16*, pp. 211-229, 1992.

18. S. Smilansky, Different Mourning Patterns and the Orphan's Utilization of his Intellectual Ability to Understand the Concept of Death, *Advances in Thanatology, 5*, pp. 39-55, 1981.

19. M. Gartley and M. Bernasconi, The Concept of Death in Children, *Journal of Genetic Psychology, 110*, pp. 71-85, 1964.

20. D. J. Schonfeld and S. Smilansky, A Cross-cultural Comparison of Israeli and American Children's Death Concepts, *Death Studies, 13*, pp. 593-604, 1989.

21. M. W. Speece and S. B. Brent, The "Adult" Concept of Irreversibility, in *Young People and Death*, J. D. Morgan (ed.), The Charles Press, Philadelphia, 1991.
22. G. M. Furth, *The Secret World of Drawings: Healing Through Art*, Sigo Press, Boston, 1988.
23. B. McIntyre, Art Therapy with Bereaved Youth, *Journal of Palliative Care*, 6:1, pp. 16-25, 1990.
24. R. Lonetto, *Children's Conceptions of Death*, Springer Publishing Company, New York, 1980.
25. E. J. Deveau, The Impact on Adolescents When a Sibling is Dying, in *The Dying and Bereaved Teenager*, J. D. Morgan (ed.), The Charles Press, Philadelphia, 1990.
26. C. A. Corr and J. N. McNeil (eds.), *Adolescence and Death*, Springer Publishing Company, New York, 1986.
27. M. Lewis, *Clinical Aspects of Child Development*, Lea and Febiger, Philadelphia, 1982.
28. D. W. Adams and E. J. Deveau, When a Brother or Sister is Dying of Cancer: The Vulnerability of the Adolescent Sibling, *Death Studies, 11*, pp. 279-285, 1987.
29. S. Fleming and R. Adolf, Helping Bereaved Adolescents: Needs and Responses, in *Adolescence and Death*, C. A. Corr and J. N. McNeil (eds.), Springer Publishing Company, New York, 1986.
30. A. Maurer, Adolescent Attitudes Toward Death, *Journal of Genetic Psychology, 105*, pp. 75-90, 1964.
31. I. E. Alexander and A. M. Adlerstein, Affective Responses to the Concept of Death in a Population of Children and Early Adolescents, *Journal of Genetic Psychology, 3*, pp. 167-177, 1958.
32. J. Bertoia, *Drawings from a Dying Child*, Routledge, London, 1993.
33. E. H. Waechter, Children's Awareness of Fatal Illness, *American Journal of Nursing, 71*, pp. 1168-1172, 1971.
34. M. Bluebond-Langner, *The Private Worlds of Dying Children*, Princeton University Press, Princeton, New Jersey, 1978.
35. H. Wass, J. L. Raup, and H. H. Sisler, Adolescence and Death on Television: A Follow-Up Study, *Death Studies, 13*, pp. 161-173, 1989.

VOLUME 1–PART B

The Influence of Society and Culture on Children and Adolescents' Perceptions and Attitudes Toward Life-Threatening Illness and Death

CHAPTER 6

Appetite for Destruction: Children and Violent Death in Popular Culture

Hannelore Wass

INTRODUCTION

Contemporary children and youth have fewer personal encounters with natural and normal death than those in previous eras: Nearly three fourths of the people who die are sixty-five years old or older. Grandparents and other older relatives often live and die in distant geographic regions making it less likely that children will attend their funerals or that children had been emotionally close to them while they were alive. Thus many children live through childhood, adolescence, and even their early adult years without having experienced a death in the family. Partly because these families do not have to deal with death, and partly because many parents still consider the whole subject inappropriate or are simply uncomfortable with it, death is hardly ever discussed with children in many homes.

How, then, do children learn the basic lessons about death? How do they learn society's attitudes, values, and orientations toward death? This is the irony: Death is abundantly present in the child's world—in the popular culture. And, this culture is a potent teacher. Contemporary Western societies are founded on the Judeo-Christian and humanistic ideology that affirms the value of life, the dignity and worth of each person, and encourages behaviors of tolerance and peaceful co-existence. These cultural values presumably underlie transactions among individuals and social institutions such as schools and professional groups. For example, care and concern for helping children with death-related issues—the subject of this volume—reflect this ideology.

Popular culture, however, does not always reflect traditional ideology, and may, in fact, express attitudes and values that are in direct conflict with it. This certainly seems to be true with respect to death. Violence is a preferred theme for entertainment which is dramatically displayed by the mass media, especially television. Because programs with themes of violence and destruction are viewed by a great many adults, by default, a great many children also become active viewers.

TELEVISION

Television is by far the most prominent mass medium. About 98 percent of American households, a total of ninety million, have at least one television set. It is like no other medium in its attractiveness, accessibility, and status, and thus has pervasive power to impact on masses of people. I do not intend to slight the valuable functions that television serves, such as providing news and various types of information, political, scientific, health, life style, cultural diversity, technology, and, of course, entertainment. The focus in this chapter, however, is on the portrayal of violent death in the media and the effect such portrayal has on children and youth.

U.S. children watch from twenty-one to twenty-eight hours of television per week, more time than for any other out-of-school activity [1]. By far the large majority of the programs children view (95%) are not specifically designed for them. More than half of all children watch prime time programs [2]. These programs contain a great deal of violence, an average of five acts per hour, or ten times as much as in real life [3].

Violent death on television is spectacular, often shown in graphic detail with close-ups of violent acts and bodily mutilation. In many programs the plot is not well developed, or the victims are criminals, so the viewer is not engaged sufficiently to develop empathy or compassion for the victim. And rarely are the pain and suffering of grief that follow death ever shown in any depth.

Children's programs are even more violent than those for adults in prime time. In an analysis and comparison of these two types of programs over two decades, Gerbner and his associates found that consistently there had been about five violent acts per hour in prime time but twenty to twenty-five in children's Saturday morning cartoons [4, 5]. These acts involved destruction of property and physical assault that caused injury and death. The argument that children do not take cartoon characters seriously is not convincing. And, it is little comfort to know that cartoon characters never stay dead very long. The message here is that nobody dies or, whatever death is, it's a temporary condition; neither is a helpful message for the young child. In addition, the child learns that violence is the answer to conflict.

The subject of television violence and children has been of interest to scholars and researchers and of concern to government officials, law makers, teachers, parents, and others, from the time broadcasting began. Violence levels have been high since measurements have been made and continue to increase. In addition, evidence of negative effects of televised and filmed violence on children and adolescents has accumulated from hundreds of studies over several decades [6-9] and from increasing numbers in the past few years [2].

Based on a review of this literature and recent testimony, the American Psychological Association Commission on Violence and Youth has reached these conclusions:

1. Frequent viewing of violence on television is correlated with increased acceptance of aggressive attitudes and behavior.
2. Viewing violence increases the fear of becoming a victim.
3. Young children's exposure to television violence can have harmful lifelong consequences.
4. Viewing violence increasingly desensitizes children to violence.
5. Viewing violence increases apathetic behavior [10].

Comstock and Paik have suggested that the influence of televised and filmed violence can be explained by three major factors: 1) non-redundancy, 2) social cognition, and 3) development [2]. When violence presented in the media does not also occur in the child's real life (is non-redundant), it influences behavior because it provides new information. Violent portrayals are dramatic and often emotional and therefore, they may be particularly compelling. On the other hand, repetitive and redundant portrayals of violence contribute to expectations and perceptions that, in effect, become scripts, scenarios, and maps (social cognition) for behavior. The developmental factor indicates that violent portrayals contribute to the acquisition of stable traits beginning early in childhood.

Even the television industry is beginning to admit its impact. A CBS executive recently said, ". . . We are not helping violence . . . We are encouraging, maybe stimulating it, maybe shaping it, but we are not the sole cause of violence!" [11].

PUBLIC POLICY

Despite all the evidence presently in the United States, no effective changes in television violence have been made, although the prospects for such change seem to be good. It may be instructive to review briefly the history of public policy-making concerning children's programming, because it illustrates the conflict that exists between public interest and the television industry.

The major legislation governing television, the Communications Act of 1934, states that television stations must serve the "public interest, convenience, and necessity," but enforcement has been minimal. While in most other Western countries governments or government-sponsored stations maintained control over quality and quantity of programming, scheduling, etc., in the United States television was considered primarily as entertainment and therefore the domain of private commercial interest [12]. Because of this commercial definition and a strong tradition of "free speech" in this country, it has been difficult to achieve any kind of regulation. In 1974 the Federal Communications Commission (FCC) specified that broadcasters must provide informative, age-specific programming for children and reduce the amount of advertising. However, the Commission agreed to let the industry make these corrections [12]. Five years later, the FCC's Children's Television Task Force evaluating the industry's progress concluded that practically no changes had been made. Nevertheless, the FCC again took no action, instead suggesting that "marketplace forces" and independent new cable channels would bring about the correction. What followed in the 1980s, was deregulation in which the few rules that did exist were abandoned.

In 1990, as a result of continued efforts of professional and citizens' advocacy groups such as the American Academy of Pediatrics, the American Psychological Association, the National Education Association, and the National Coalition on Television Violence, the U.S. Congress passed the Television Violence Act. Under this law, broadcasters had until the fall of 1993 to voluntarily lower the levels of violence in prime time programs. In addition, the Children's Television Education Act was passed to regulate advertising. A third act passed in 1990 removed antitrust restraint allowing the broadcasting industry to collaborate in reducing violence [12]. The threat of legislative action by Congress has so far brought only promises from the leaders of the industry [11].

It is time for action. New technologies, especially the introduction of basic cable and VCR, have greatly increased access to all types of media content by young viewers. Already nearly half of American households have basic cable and VCR in addition to television. While independent channels offer many new adult programs, the expected increase in quality programs for children, based on the "market force" principle mentioned above, unfortunately has not happened [2, 12].

VCR AND FEATURE FILMS

Anyone visiting a video rental store can find a large variety of materials including pornographic and violent fare, usually prominently displayed. Although rental stores say they do not rent inappropriate materials to minors, few are believed to check their identification. It has been shown that adolescents rent sexually violent and explicit tapes and find them compelling [13]. It has also been shown that any restrictions or prescriptions by parents that one might have expected, have not occurred. Parents are only slightly concerned that sons may seek out obscene, pornographic, and savagely violent material [14-16]. It has been shown that youngsters who use VCR's are more likely to have problems with their parents or peers [2]. A video titled "Faces of Death," that came on the market in the mid-1980s, became popular with adolescents who rented it and apparently held parties to see who would get "grossed out" the most. The tape contains lengthy footage and closeups of various kinds of physical assault and mutilation including death in the electric chair, by hanging, cannibalism, and satanic practice involving a human body. The questions one inevitably asks when viewing such fare is, "What does it teach children about the dignity and value we assign to persons and to life? What sort of emotions are aroused in young viewers and how do they handle them?"

There is also an abundance of feature films in which violent death is the major theme and in which killing is glamorized. Many adults in our society seem addicted to such entertainment. Not only does the camera focus compulsively on the acts of violence and on bodily mutilation, but the deaths often occur in large quantities. In the movie *Rambo,* there are seventy explosions involving individuals or groups and forty-four specific killings; a death occurs every 2.1 minutes [17]. In sequels to popular films there are also increasingly larger numbers of violent deaths. For instance, in *Die Hard II*, the body count is up from eighteen to 264. A number of films are custom-made for the young and have brought fortunes to enterprising businessmen.

Adolescents are both frightened and fascinated by grossly violent movies, as well as by films dealing with the occult [18, 19]. Unfortunately there are few studies on the effect of these newer types of violent feature films on children. It is known that they go to see them. Many parents even take their young children to see them, apparently not aware of the negative effects. By and large, the public seems to be less disturbed by violence than by sexual explicitness in film and television. The existing rating system applies to sexually explicit material, not to violence.

TOYS

There is also a link between television and toys. The deregulation of broadcasting in the 1980s removed rules that had been designed to protect children, including regulations with respect to advertising during children's programs. As a result, not only was the amount of time devoted to advertising during children's programs increased, but in addition, entire programs were built around certain products, a practice called "program-length advertising." Children's vulnerability to advertising has long been established, as has the effectiveness of advertising on children's desire to own the products, their frustration when they do not receive them, and the rate at which children persuade parents to purchase them [2]. The use of more advertising, especially program-length advertising, resulted in soaring sales of toys with television exposure. For example, the "GI Joe Modern Army Action Toys" consisting of over fifty items, have become a leading toy line. Similarly, sales of the "He-Man" action figures, tied to the "Masters-of-the-Universe" television program, doubled in a matter of a few years. In 1984 alone, Mattell sold thirty-five million "He-Man" figures, nearly 95,000 per day. Smaller toy companies, that could not compete in the television-dominated market, disappeared. Playskool and Milton Bradley, for example, were bought by Hasbro, the maker of the "GI Joe" toys. Between 1984 and 1990, the sale of war toys rose 500 percent. For a number of years the best-selling single toy during the Christmas season has been a war toy [20].

Toys and games are another cultural force, another medium for socializing children, predominantly boys, for violence. Playing with aggressive toys familiarizes children with the many ways people can kill one another. It also makes such action appear easy, and without consequence. It would be naive to think that such practice has no influence on children's attitudes and values. It is interesting to note here that almost half of all American households possess guns [10]. Thousands of people including children die annually from gunshot wounds, most of them accidentally during play.

ROCK LYRICS

Hate, violence, and murder are also themes in the songs of certain types of rock music, especially heavy metal and rap. Rock music has been a "counter-culture" phenomenon. In its forty-year history it has provided a forum for adolescents to assert their growing autonomy from adult figures. Heavy metal and rap are recent variations of the general rock and roll music form. Sex, love, drugs, antiwar protest, and a number of social issues have been themes in the past and continue to be today. However, since the 1980s, there is a new dimension to a number of songs—a stance of meanness, destructiveness, and assertion of power not found in previous eras. Their targets are women, ethnic and religious minorities, foreigners, and authority figures. While other, softer forms of rock music continue to be most popular among older children and adolescents, a significant minority of them are attracted to this other music and the songs. In two studies nearly a fifth of the adolescents said they were fans of either the songs that promote murder, suicide, or satanic practices, or the bands that produce the songs [21, 22]. Furthermore, this ratio increased to nearly 50 percent in a survey of residents in a juvenile detention center [23].

Heavy metal groups that produced hateful and destructive songs in the 1980s, such as "Metallica," "Iron Maiden," "Motley Crue," and "AC/DC," have become popular. The group "Guns N' Roses" sold fourteen million copies of their 1987 debut album *Appetite for Destruction*. More recent releases have met with similar success. Whatever the musical value of this band's sound may be, the lyrics are violent, sexist, and racist. These are some lines from the band's songs: ". . . I used to love her but I had to kill her; police and niggers, that's right, get out of my way; immigrants and faggots . . . come to our country . . . spread some f— disease" [24]. The following lyric is from a recent album by a popular group, the "Geto Boys": "She begged me not to kill her, I gave her a rose/then slit her throat, watched her shake till her eyes closed; had sex with the corpse before I left her/and drew my name on the wall like Helter Skelter" [25]. A song by the band "Slasher" includes these lines: "No apparent motive/just kill and kill again/survive my brutal slashing/ I'll hunt you till the end." The band "Venom" in their 1985 album *Welcome to Hell* produced these lyrics: ". . . I am possessed by all that is evil/the death of your God I demand/I spit at the virgin you worship/ and sit at Lord Satan's right hand" [21].

Professional and citizens' groups have worked to protect children from such material. Since 1985 the "Parents' Music Resource Center," begun by Tipper Gore, wife of Vice-President Gore, and others have worked to inform parents of the existence of such lyrics and to persuade the music industry to self monitor their products and to introduce a system of labeling or rating on album covers. (This group has *not* promoted censorship as some of the industry representatives and industry apologists have charged.) From time to time, some record stores and large chains, such as Eckerds and Walmart, have pulled certain albums off their shelves, and other groups have applied pressure with some success. For example, when the rapper "Ice-T" published the song *Copkiller*, police organizations protested, record stores pulled the album that contained the song, and Warner-Time canceled the rapper's contract, citing "creative differences." A number of states have been considering legislation to force the music industry to introduce labeling. One of the states is Pennsylvania. The suggested label would say: "Warning: may contain explicit lyrics descriptive of or advocating one or more of the following: suicide, sodomy, incest, bestiality, sadomasochism, sexual activity in a violent context, murder, morbid violence, or use of illegal drugs or alcohol" [26]. It is doubtful that the industry will print such lengthy labels, although a case could be made for it by citing the new regulation for food labeling.

There are people who question the need for concern about rock lyrics. They share their thinking in teen magazines and fan club newsletters. These people argue the following: religious fundamentalists, politically extreme rightists, the older generation, and otherwise "uptight" people have always tried to curb rock songs, so disregard them; this music is pretty innocent; it represents a phase young people go through; the lyrics do not mean what they say; it's all a big joke to get adults riled up; and, this music is for singing and dancing.

Of course, no study can ever show that a rock song is the single, solitary reason why a young person commits suicide or kills. No respectable researcher would make such a claim. But what if a young person listens to a hundred such songs over and over; watches a hundred television programs, music videos, and home videos; lives in poverty in an unstable family; drinks or is on drugs; and is a school dropout? The problem is one of multi-faceted and cumulative exposure of "at risk" youth and few interceding forces.

The subject of explicit rock lyrics is perhaps even more deeply controversial than that of televised and filmed aggression. One side argues that a person's right to free speech, that is, an artist's right to free artistic expression, is threatened by rating and labeling and this amounts to a type of censorship. Health professionals and other advocacy groups take the opposing position which considers young people's right to personal safety and constructive behavior, and society's obligation to safeguard and promote it. With these concerns pitted against one another, many decide in favor of social responsibility. Meanwhile the entertainment industry maintains its right to profit.

It is interesting to note the merging of the news and entertainment industry into super corporations. In 1991, for example, Time and Warner regrouped, joined by two Japanese companies, Toshiba and C. Itoh. Together this conglomerate owns a large share of the publishing, television, cable, film, and music market (1990 revenues of

$2.25 billion) [27]. With such consolidation comes much cross-marketing. When a band such as "Guns N' Roses" becomes a success virtually overnight, one is tempted to speculate that the degree to which its music reflects the Zeitgeist of America's young people is smaller than the degree to which they are manipulated by carefully orchestrated and timed promotion.

It will remain the task of future social and behavioral scientists to find answers to this question and the more general question concerning the violent tenor in popular culture and its pervasive effects on younger generations.

GENDER STEREOTYPING

When discussing violence in the popular culture one would be remiss not to address the question of gender stereotypes. Whenever aggression and violence are presented, the main actors are males. Males are the perpetrators, and women and children are often the victims. Thus, when children are bombarded with violence, they are also reinforced in traditional gender stereotypes. Longitudinal studies have shown that children who watch a lot of television are more strongly gender-stereotyped than those who watch less [12]. In a natural experiment, Williams studied three communities in British Columbia before and after they had access to television [28]. He found that the introduction of television in the community increased sex stereotyping in children.

Though our society has made significant progress toward gender equity and both women and men's groups are attempting to redefine their gender identities in a changing world, television clings tenaciously to the old stereotypes.

To place the issue of violence and pop culture into the larger context, it is useful to consider two additional aspects, the reporting of news and the incidence of real violence in the child's environment.

NEWS

Increasingly, television has become the major source of news information for young adult groups, thereby determining to a large extent how they perceive what is happening in the world [2]. From numerous studies it can be concluded that this applies to children as well. The majority of them believe that they get most of their information about public events from television and rank it above teachers, parents, peers, and other media [29, 30]. A substantial number of children watch the news. Between 30 to 40 percent of children in grades four, eight, and eleven watch national news daily, somewhat more watch local news [1]. As children get older, they increasingly watch the news on television. There is no shortage of news on television. However, because of the nature of the medium and television broadcasters' definition of, and policies on, what is newsworthy, there is a consistent bias toward reporting negative and spectacular events. Disasters, accidents, and acts of violence are the stuff that make good news. Because of instant communication around the globe, there is much violent news to report daily. There are horrors of genocide, war, terrorism, hunger, and deprivation brought into our homes in relentless succession. But when this is not offset with representation of the many things that are joyful, constructive, and good in the world, it is not surprising that many heavy viewers come to see the world as a mean and violent place [2].

VIOLENCE IN THE HOME AND COMMUNITY

For many people it is, in fact, a violent world in which they live. Increasing violence in the home, on the street, and in the neighborhood affects a substantial number of children and adolescents directly and personally, especially in inner-city ghettos. The rate of deaths by homicide has increased most dramatically in the age group fifteen to twenty-four years [31]. Homicide is now the second highest cause of death for this age group and has been the primary cause of death for Afro-American males for more than a decade.

Many children are victims because they have witnessed deadly violence and are living with the trauma of such experiences. For example, in a study of grade eight students in Chicago, it was found that three-fourths had seen someone robbed, stabbed, shot, or killed [10]. Many more children live in constant fear for their own lives. In a recent survey the Centers for Disease Control found that one in five high school students had carried a weapon in the month before the survey, some admitted they carried a gun [32]. Many large school systems in the country have installed metal detectors and are trying to obtain funds so they can employ security guards.

Not surprisingly, destructive behavior among young people has also been rising at accelerated rates [10]. Seventeen percent of all arrests for violent crimes are youths and this figure may be an underestimate [33, 34]. Although still infrequent, between 1985 and 1991, arrests made for homicide among seventeen-year-old adolescents increased by 121 percent. The rate increase was almost double for fifteen to sixteen-year-old teenagers [35].

While we do not have a complete understanding of the causes, manifestations, and control of violence among youth, factors involved in patterns that put them at risk are already known. They include poverty, abuse in childhood, violence in the popular culture, violence in the environment, unstable family life, lack of positive role models, access to weapons, drug and alcohol abuse, failure in school, and involvement in antisocial groups. Violence in the popular culture is a part of these children's lives and contributes importantly to aggressive behavior, but also to fear, apathy, and misperception.

SOME SUGGESTIONS FOR INTERVENTION

There are many ways adults can mediate and intervene. Some thoughts and ideas are offered here.

A number of organizations offer resources for parents and teachers that may be helpful. The group, "Action for Children's Television" (20 Universal Road, Cambridge, MA 02138), distributes books, pamphlets, films, and other material to guide children's television viewing. The organization, "Children's Creative Response to Conflict" (Box 271, Nyack, NY 10960), publishes teaching and parenting materials to help children learn to communicate, cooperate, and deal constructively with conflict. For additional organizations please refer to the books by Carlsson-Paige and Levin [20] and Leviton [36].

Suggestions for Parents

Parents are the most significant people in children's lives. One of their primary functions is to help their children learn basic facts and adopt positive and constructive attitudes toward themselves, others, life, and the world. Today's children are flooded with stimulation, data, and other material of all sorts. Without parental mediation and guidance it is often difficult and confusing for them to make sense of, and to evaluate what is presented to them. It is even more difficult for them to come through it all with optimism, positive attitudes, and pro-social behavior. Parents can provide experiences that counteract the violent tenor in the popular culture today. Below are just a few suggestions in this direction:

1. Limit the types of programs children may watch.
2. Limit the number of hours of watching per day.
3. Determine the times during which children can watch television.
4. Provide and encourage alternative activities such as arts, crafts, hobbies, reading, and non-violent games.

5. Watch programs with children. Counteract violent messages by expressing disapproval and pointing out the fictional nature of the program.
6. Discuss alternative ways to resolve conflict.
7. Watch the news with children. Provide comfort and perspective.
8. Be a role model.

What Teachers Can Do

Increasingly, schools have been asked to fill needs that are not met in the home. The suggestions that follow, however, are not meant as such replacements. They are educational suggestions to help children become more informed about the media they use. Teachers can teach "media literacy" in units, modules, discussions, debates or in other ways. Following are some suggested topics:

1. Television program production, including script, actors, props, cameras, camera angles, background music, etc.
2. Types of programs, rating systems, determination of time slots, etc.
3. Television advertising including objectives, relationship between the commercial and the program, product disclaimers, expense, frequency, methods of persuasion, deceptive advertising, and individuals' power to resist, etc.
4. Cooperation and conflict resolution, including negotiation and mediation.
5. Management of anger and frustration.

Contributions by Caregivers

As the health care field moves closer toward a philosophy of preventive health, and violence is viewed as preventable, caregivers increasingly focus on this complex issue. Within this larger frame of reference, they can fill an important need concerning mass media. They can provide information and understanding about the negative effects of media violence on children's attitudes, social perception, motivations, and behavior, and recommend healthful alternatives. They can organize and hold public information lectures, seminars, workshops, and similar activities. Caregivers can add their support to existing advocacy groups or initiate their own. Finally, they can work with parents and children at the clinical level.

REFERENCES

1. S. G. Timmer, J. Eccles, and K. O'Brien, How Children Use Time, in *Time, Goods, and Well-Being*, F. T. Juster and F. P. Stafford (eds.), Institute for Social Research, University of Michigan, Ann Arbor, 1985.
2. G. Comstock and H. Paik, *Television and the American Child*, Academic Press, New York, 1991.
3. M. Morgan, Cultivation Analysis, in *International Encyclopedia of Communication, Vol. I*, E. Barnouw (ed.), Oxford University Press, New York, 1988.
4. G. Gerbner and L. Gross, Living with Television: The Violence Profile, in *Journal of Communication, 26*, pp. 172-199, 1976.
5. G. Gerbner, L. Gross, M. Morgan, and N. Signorielli, The "Mainstreaming" of America: Violence Profile N. 11, *Journal of Communication, 30*, pp. 10-29, 1980.
6. Surgeon General's Scientific Advisory Committee, Television and Growing Up: The Impact of Televised Violence, Committee Report on Television and Social Behavior, U.S. Government Printing Office, Washington, D.C., 1972.
7. D. Pearl, L. Bouthilet, and J. Lazar, *Television and Behavior: Ten Years of Scientific Progress and Implications for the Eighties*, Vol. 2, Technical Reviews, U.S. Government Printing Office, Washington, D.C., 1982.
8. J. L. Singer and D. G. Singer, Some Hazards of Growing Up in a Television Environment: Children's Aggression and Restlessness, in *Television as a Social Issue, Applied Psychology Annual*, Vol. 2, S. Oskamp (ed.), Sage, Newbury Park, California, pp. 172-188, 1987.
9. E. L. Palmer, *Television and America's Children: A Crisis of Neglect*, Oxford University Press, New York, 1988.
10. American Psychological Association Commission on Violence and Youth, *Violence and Youth: Psychology's Response*, Vol. 1, Summary Report, Washington, D.C., 1993.
11. P. Hefner and K. P. Karla, When Violence Entertains, *Gainesville Sun*, May 23, 1993.
12. A. C. Huston et al., *Big World, Small Screen: The Role of Television in American Society*, University of Nebraska Press, Lincoln, 1992.
13. R. W. Kubey and R. Larson, The Use and Experience of the New Video Media among Children and Young Adolescents, *Communication Research, 17*, pp. 107-130, 1990.
14. B. S. Greenberg and C. Heeter, VCR's and Young People, *American Behavioral Scientist, 30*, pp. 509-521, 1987.
15. W. Y. Kim, S. J. Baran, and K. Massey, Impact of the VCR on Control of Television Viewing, *Journal of Broadcasting & Electronic Media, 32*, pp. 351-357, 1988.
16. C. A. Lin and D. J. Atkin, Parental Mediation and Rulemaking for Adolescent Use of Television and VCR, *Journal of Broadcasting and Electronic Media, 33*, pp. 53-67, 1989.

17. M. C. Kearl, *Endings: A Sociology of Death and Dying*, Oxford University Press, New York, 1989.

18. H. Wass, J. M. Stillion, and A. F. Fattah, Exploding Images: Gifted Children's View of Violence and Death on Television, in *Death: Completion and Discovery*, C. A. Corr and R. A. Pacholski (eds.), Association for Death Education and Counseling, Lakewood, Ohio, 1987.

19. H. Wass, J. L. Raup, and H. H. Sisler, Adolescence and Death on Television: A Follow-Up Study, *Death Studies, 13,* pp. 161-173, 1989.

20. N. Carlsson-Paige and D. E. Levin, *Who's Calling the Shots?*, New Society Publishers, Philadelphia, Pennsylvania, 1990.

21. H. Wass et al., Adolescents' Interest in and Views of Destructive Themes in Rock Music, *Omega, 19,* pp. 177-186, 1988.

22. H. Wass, M. D. Miller, and R. G. Stevenson, Factors Affecting Adolescents' Behavior and Attitudes toward Destructive Rock Lyrics, *Death Studies, 13,* pp. 287-303, 1989.

23. H. Wass, M. D. Miller, and C. A. Redditt, Adolescents and Destructive Themes in Rock Music: A Follow-Up, *Omega, 23,* pp. 199-206, 1991.

24. J. Queenan, Misfit Metalheads, *Time*, pp. 80-83, Sept. 30, 1991.

25. P. Plagen, M. Miller, D. Foote, and E. Yoffe, Violence in Our Culture, *Newsweek*, pp. 46-52, April 1, 1991.

26. A. McGraw, Record-labelling Issue Rises on National Charts, *Gainesville Sun*, March 4, 1990.

27. Associated Press, Japanese Firms Join with Time Warner, *Gainesville Sun*, October 30, 1991.

28. T. D. Williams (ed.), *The Impact of Television: A Natural Experiment in Three Communities*, Academic Press, New York, 1986.

29. D. G. Drew and B. Reeves, Children's Learning from a Television News Cast, *Journalism Quarterly, 61,* pp. 83-88, 1984.

30. J. M. Meadowcroft, Family Communication Pattern and Political Development: The Child's Role, *Communication Research, 13,* pp. 603-624, 1986.

31. R. K. Lore and L. A. Schultz, Control of Human Aggression, *American Psychologist, 48,* pp. 16-25, 1993.

32. Centers for Disease Control, Weapon-Carrying among High School Students, *Journal of the American Medical Association, 266,* p. 2342, 1991.

33. C. P. Ewing, *Kids Who Kill*, Lexington Press, Lexington, Massachusetts, 1990.

34. B. Cantrowitz, Wild in the Streets, *Newsweek*, pp. 40-46, August 2, 1993.

35. F. Bayles, Crime Rising Despite Drop in Teen Males, *Gainesville Sun*, October 15, 1992.

36. D. Leviton (ed.), *Horrendous Death and Health: Toward Action,* Taylor and Francis, New York, 1991.

CHAPTER 7

American Children and Desert Storm: Impressions of the Gulf Conflict

Gerry R. Cox, Bernard J. Vanden Berk,
Ronald J. Fundis, and Patrick J. McGinnis

The terrors of war affect everyone, but how does war affect children? Are children too young to understand war? What does war mean to them? While studies addressing children and war are sparse, the issues within this study have received much attention. If death and separation are the focal points of an investigation, the attitudes of children toward war would be extremely negative. If, however, children focus upon different aspects of the war and if they respond individually to war itself, they may not all possess a negative attitude to war. It is expected that children are responding more individually to war and that gender may have a decided impact on their attitudes.

A considerable body of empirical research has documented that gender differences in attitudes toward war, violence, and aggressiveness do, in fact, exist. Goertzel [1], Kriesberg and Klein [2], Putney and Middleton [3], Smith [4], Maccoby and Jacklin [5], and Mead [6], suggest that this attitudinal difference is learned. This leads to the conclusion that the more a person internalizes these societal and cultural messages, the more apparent these attitudes will become. Children are quickly "genderized" by their socializers, learning particular roles and becoming increasingly stereotypical of a gender as they grow [7-11]. For example, aggressiveness and violence are generally promoted more in male children, while passivity and emotionalism are usually promoted more in female children. Pierce and Edwards discovered that when children were allowed the freedom to express themselves creatively toward conflict resolution without environmental pressures, they would often demonstrate stereotypical sex roles [12]. Males used more violent resolution, and females used more reasoning and analysis.

Each of these past studies investigated the learned stereotypical sex role that children are channeled into by their socializers. Yet, each deals only with issues that do not approach the emotional quagmire of war. War is confusing and filled with undefinable concepts and unanswerable questions.

Zur and Morrison looked at gender attitudes toward war in adults and found that support for a war often depended upon how it was justified [13]. For females to endorse the war, the justification was most likely for reasons of morality or for family cohesiveness. Males were more likely to support war through rationalization.

RESEARCH PERSPECTIVE

In the case of the Gulf War, thousands of children's parents and relatives were forced to leave with the possibility that they might never return. Obviously, this had immense impact on these children, and yet, could stereotypical sex roles still alter seemingly pure emotional responses to war? It was hypothesized that children would indeed fall subject to gender roles in response to war. First, males would be more likely to support the war and identify with its violence. Secondly, females would be more likely to oppose the war and respond to the emotional issues surrounding it. The third hypothesis was that, as grade level increases, violent and aggressive pictures will increase for both genders.

METHODOLOGY

Data Source

The questionnaire (see Appendix A) was designed to create an opportunity to estimate the effects of the war at a very basic level on young children. The questionnaire sought descriptive words, a drawing expressing the child's thoughts on the war, an explanation of the drawing, and the name, sex, and grade of each student. For the descriptive words, students were given directions and five blanks that asked for any five words that "you think and feel about the Persian Gulf War." These instructions were read by each teacher along with the side statement, "there are no right or wrong answers." Following the five descriptive words was a blank space to draw a picture about what each student thought or felt about the Persian Gulf War. A few lines were provided to explain (tell about) the picture. All teachers involved were visited personally and instructed on how to handle the survey. These rules were stressed: 1) no oral responses to questions that might suggest answers (i.e., how do I spell Saddam?); 2) emphasize that spelling does not matter; 3) if a child needs help with spelling, it should be done quietly on a one-on-one basis; 4) under no circumstances should a question be explained or example answers given; and 5) do not allow the students to look at one another's papers.

The survey was conducted on February 1, 1991, in Valley View Elementary Public School, Ashwaubenon, Wisconsin, to first, third, and fifth grade students. Soon after, it was administered at St. Joseph's parochial elementary school in Hays, Kansas. February 1 was a few days after the huge oil spill was discovered in the Persian Gulf. All the teachers involved reported that the survey worked well and the students required little help.

The convenience sample was not random. The emphasis was on accessing different age/grade levels in a pilot project. Table 1 provides the profile of the respondents. Four hundred and eight (408) questionnaires were filled out in Ashwaubenon and eighty-four in Hays. The questionnaires were divided as follows: 145 to grade one students, 128 to students in grade three, and 219 to grade five students which presents a fairly even distribution toward age. The schools were not random with respect to race, wealth, or religion. In fact, St. Joseph's Elementary School is a Catholic Parochial School. All students in class

Table 1. Profile of Respondents

	Percent	Frequency
Location of School (*n* = 492)		
Ashwaubenon, Wisconsin	82.9	408
Hays, Kansas	17.1	84
Gender (*n* = 492)		
Male	44.3	218
Female	55.7	274
Grade of Respondent (*n* = 492)		
First Grade	29.5	145
Third Grade	26.0	128
Fifth Grade	44.5	219

that day participated in the survey and no prior questioning took place. The purpose was to take a quick look at children's attitudes toward war in the most convenient setting—schools.

Data Analysis

Coding was established using a content analysis methodology which permitted the identification of trends within the responses. Codes were also determined for city, sex, and grade level. Next, codes were developed after taking samples of words used in the first question. The method involved coding types of responses into common and easily definable categories. This was an attempt to measure their understanding of the war, what issues they dealt with, and what influenced their beliefs. The categories were as follows:

1. Abstract words devoid of emotion or easily conceptualized meaning (i.e., war, like, very, etc.)
2. Leaders in the war
3. Words associated with people in the war (i.e., soldiers, units, operations, etc.)
4. Words associated with people not in the war (i.e., friends, family, etc.)
5. Terms involving violence or descriptive of war (i.e., killing, shooting, blowing up, etc.)
6. Words that express hope (i.e., pray, wish, hope, etc.)
7. Terms that name a geographical location (i.e., home, Iraq, USA, etc.)
8. Words that express positive emotions (i.e., love, happy, etc.)
9. Words that express negative emotions (i.e., hate, sad, mad, angry, etc.)
10. Terms naming, describing, or dealing with weaponry (i.e., guns, bombs, SCUDS, etc.)
11. Words pertaining to the environment (i.e., sand, oil, desert, etc.)
12. Words that exhibit confusion (i.e., why, hyper, etc.)
13. Missing value.

Next the hand-drawn pictures were coded, which again demanded a wide range of topics and a "yes it is there, no it is not" type of judgment (see Appendix B for samples of completed questionnaires and drawings). The statement following each of the sample drawings was used as a part of the picture and was not coded separately. Each respondent's drawing was judged as to whether or not action was present, weapons were present, people were present and of what type (self, others, or soldiers), or an opinion was presented clearly (and what it was). In addition, expressions on people's faces were tallied by what emotion was being shown (anger, sadness, happiness, etc.).

Each phase of the coding was extremely difficult due to the lack of legibility, incorrect spelling, and inability of the young children to articulate their thoughts, especially in a drawing. Coding of the drawings posed constant problems in making clear definitions of the individual's intent and purpose, and this impeded consistent recording. Several surveys were completely unreadable, and although these presented just as much feeling as the others, they were impossible to code. Other drawings had parts crossed out or were totally confusing as to a theme or even what it was intended to represent. The drawings ranged from elaborate emotional pictures to completely abstract art.

RESULTS

The findings indicated that students documented detailed thoughts throughout the completed questionnaires. All surveyed students had at least some feelings about the war, most did not have enough room to express themselves. Their responses revealed well-formed ideas about the war, as well as diverse opinions. Gender differences were very obvious as were differences between ages. Females identified much more with individual people and emotions. Males, on the other hand, displayed more aggressiveness with guns and war scenes. The differences, however, increased noticeably with grade level.

The results basically conformed to the hypothetical beliefs previously noted. The data revealed a strong and significant trend (using Chi-square analysis) with sex and grade on the descriptive word sections ($p < .01$). The statistical analysis followed SPSS format using city, sex, and grade as independent variables. Since Tables 2 and 3 consisted of the many topics investigated, it diluted the statistical significance of the more major variables such as violent terms to gender, positive and negative emotional terms to gender, and violent terms to grade. The analysis of the pictures offers perhaps the best evidence to support the first two hypotheses.

Table 2, Overall Descriptive Words by Sex, demonstrates the obvious difference between males and females, especially in negative emotions toward the war.

Throughout the analysis the sex differences convincingly support the first hypothesis. Boys are significantly more likely to name weapons, give violent terms as answers, and not react as negatively to the war. Girls are much more likely to identify with the people associated with the war, as well as respond with more hope and a more positive attitude. The total descriptive words to sex is not statistically

Table 2. Overall Descriptive Words by Sex

Word Codes	Male (n = 1090)	Female (n = 1365)
Abstract Words	24 (2.2%)	37 (2.4%)
Leaders in the War	65 (6.0%)	52 (3.8%)
People in the War	84 (7.7%)	103 (7.5%)
People not in the War	19 (1.7%)	35 (2.6%)
Violent Terms	199 (18.3%)	201 (14.7%)
Words Expressing Hope	46 (4.2%)	84 (6.2%)
Places	43 (3.9%)	20 (1.5%)
Positive Emotions	23 (2.1%)	63 (4.6%)
Negative Emotions	336 (30.8%)	558 (40.9%)
Weapons	152 (13.9%)	124 (9.1%)
Environment	27 (2.5%)	26 (1.9%)
Confusion Words	15 (1.4%)	26 (2.6%)

$\chi^2 = 34.9228$, $df = 24$, $p < .02$.

significant, although the aforementioned alone are ($p < .01$). In the analysis of the drawings, sex was highly significant in predicting whether action would be present in the picture ($p < .01$), or a weapon ($p < .01$), or that males would draw a picture more often with war (more than 3 out of 4 tested) as its themes ($p < .01$). Interestingly, the girls significantly ($p < .01$) drew pictures of themselves or others, whereas the boys were more likely to draw soldiers. There was probably an expression on the face of the people in the drawings by girls (82.1%), while boys most often left the faces expressionless ($p < .01$).

Table 3, Overall Descriptive Words by Grade, reveals a decrease in negative emotion corresponding to higher grade. In addition, the findings on Table 3 add support to the third hypothesis by specifically illustrating that there is a steady, dramatic increase in the word codes for violent terms and weapons. In other words, it is much more likely that a child will report violent terms or weapons as he or she grows older ($p < .01$).

Grade level was also significant in all the comparisons. Surprisingly grade was perhaps the most consistent predictor of the three. Throughout all the questionnaires, as the grade level increased emotional reactions decreased while tolerance of the war and representation of violence and weapons increased. It seems as though the maturation process is one of "innocence lost."

Table 3. Overall Descriptive Words by Grade

Word Codes	First Grade (n = 725)		Third Grade (n = 640)		Fifth Grade (n = 1095)	
Abstract Words	24	(2.8%)	24	(3.7%)	18	(1.6%)
Leaders in the War	4	(0.6%)	31	(4.8%)	82	(7.5%)
People in the War	42	(5.8%)	53	(8.3%)	92	(8.4%)
People not in the War	14	(1.9%)	9	(1.4%)	31	(2.8%)
Violent Terms	48	(6.6%)	121	(18.9%)	231	(21.1%)
Words Expressing Hope	55	(7.5%)	34	(5.3%)	41	(3.7%)
Places	6	(0.8%)	22	(3.3%)	35	(3.2%)
Positive Emotions	39	(5.4%)	21	(3.3%)	27	(2.5%)
Negative Emotions	34	(4.7%)	178	(27.8%)	319	(29.1%)
Weapons	401	(55.3%)	103	(16.1%)	154	(14.1%)
Environment	8	(1.1%)	22	(3.4%)	23	(2.1%)
Confusion Words	16	(2.2%)	13	(2.0%)	22	(2.0%)

$\chi^2 = 81.478$, $df = 24$, $p < .01$.

DISCUSSION

There are predictable and grave results of war. First, there is the loss of human life and its effects; and second, there are the psychological effects of being in war (as dramatically illustrated by the consequences of the Viet Nam War). These after-effects, however, are first-hand components of war, but there are still other more subtle effects that tend to be disregarded by the public. One of these is the effects of war on our children. It became quite obvious during the mass mobilization of the Gulf War that children were being affected indelibly by the crisis. To truly comprehend and measure children's reactions poses a problem. Many of the thoughts, emotions, and components involved with war are difficult for adults to express, let alone for children. This study took a look at those difficult emotional subjects. Through the basic drawings and writings of grade school children, their deepest fears and beliefs about war surfaced. The findings of this research appear somewhat frightening because they indicate that, perhaps, children are being taught to be more tolerant of violence. This in turn, tends to suggest that they will support another war. This study found differences in gender toward war and a major difference by grade and attitudes toward war.

On the other hand, however, these findings should not be surprising. As one ages and receives more master messages, in-group attitudes become increasingly salient. This is one of the classical empirical and theoretical cornerstones of anthropology and sociology.

This research seems to be valuable and somewhat heuristic in nature. Although statistical significance was achieved, the sample was small and non-random. In this study, coding presented the greatest challenge. A re-coding would probably find new facts, as well as clarify the existing data and statistical analysis. Perhaps the authors underrated the varieties of attitudes and emotions that the children expressed in their drawings. Further research and manipulation of these facts and drawings could well produce findings of even greater interest. Hopefully, another war will not come along to offer that opportunity.

REFERENCES

1. C. J. Goertzel, The Gender Gaps: Family Income and Twenty Political Opinions, *Journal of Political and Military Sociology, 11*, pp. 109-222, 1983.
2. L. Kriesberg and R. Klein, Change in Public Support for U.S. Military Spending, *Journal of Conflict Resolution, 24*, pp. 79-111, 1980.
3. S. Putney and R. Middleton, Some Factors associated with Student Acceptance or Rejection of War, *American Sociological Review, 27*, pp. 655-677, 1962.
4. T. W. Smith, Polls: Gender and Attitudes Towards Violence, *Public Opinion Quarterly, 18*, pp. 384-396, 1984.
5. E. M. Maccoby and C. N. Jacklin, *The Psychology of Sex Differences*, Stanford University Press, Stanford, California, 1978.
6. M. Mead, *Sex and Temperament in Three Primitive Societies*, Morrow Quill Paperbacks, New York, 1980. (Original work published 1935.)
7. C. L. Martin and C. F. Halverson Jr., A Schematic Processing Model of Sex Typing and Stereotyping in Children, *Child Development, 52*, pp. 1119-1134, 1981.
8. D. Kuhn, S. C. Nash, and L. Brucken, Sex Role Concepts of Two and Three-year Olds, *Child Development, 49*, pp. 445-451, 1978.
9. R. J. Barry and A. Barry, Stereotyping of Sex Roles in Preschool Kindergarten Children, *Psychological Reports, 38*, pp. 948-950, 1976.
10. S. Fling and M Manosevitz, Sex Typing in Nursery School: Children's Play Interests, *Developmental Psychology, 7*, pp. 146-152, 1972.
11. R. Muller and S. Goldberg, Why William Doesn't Want a Doll: Preschools' Expectations of Adult Behavior toward Girls and Boys, *Merrill Palmer Quarterly, 26*, pp. 240-259, 1988.
12. K. Pierce and E. Edwards, Children's Construction of Fantasy Stories: Gender Differences in Conflict Resolution Strategies, *Sex Roles, 18*:7/8, pp. 393-399, 1988.
13. O. Zur and A. Morrison, Gender and War: Reexamining Attitudes, *American Journal of Orthopsychiatry, 59*:4, pp. 528-533, 1989.

APPENDIX A: Questionnaire

Name _____   Boy _____   Girl _____

Teacher _____

You have thoughts and feelings about the <u>Persian Gulf War</u>.

Write 5 words that come to mind when you think and feel
about the <u>Persian Gulf War</u>.

     1.

     2.   There are no "right" or

     3.   "wrong" answers.

     4.

     5.

Draw a picture that shows what you think or feel about the <u>Persian Gulf War</u>.

(Only use a pencil)

Tell about your picture

APPENDIX B

Name   Boy __X__   Girl _____

Teacher

You have thoughts and feelings about the <u>Persian Gulf War</u>.

Write 5 words that come to mind when you think and feel
about the <u>Persian Gulf War</u>.

1. _____ *guns* _____

2. _____ *Peple* _____   There are no "right" or

3. _____ *Sad* _____   "wrong" answers.

4. _____ *Fite* _____

5. _____ *Prdy* _____

Draw a picture that shows what you think or feel about the <u>Persian Gulf War</u>.

(Only use a pencil)

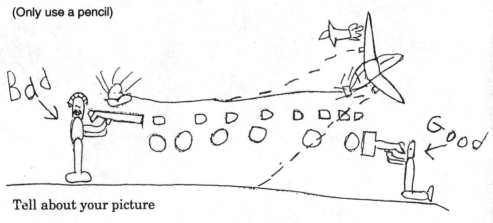

Tell about your picture

APPENDIX B (Cont'd.)

Name _____   Boy _____   Girl ✓_____

Teacher _____

You have thoughts and feelings about the <u>Persian Gulf War</u>.

Write 5 words that come to mind when you think and feel
about the <u>Persian Gulf War</u>.

1. Sad

2. Sad

3. Saad

4. Sad

5. Bad

There are no "right" or
"wrong" answers.

Draw a picture that shows what you think or feel about the <u>Persian Gulf War</u>.

(Only use a pencil)

Tell about your picture _____

Sad   Sad

Sad   Sad

Sad   Sad

APPENDIX B (Cont'd.)

Name   Boy __X__ Girl _____

Teacher

You have thoughts and feelings about the <u>Persian Gulf War</u>.

Write 5 words that come to mind when you think and feel
about the <u>Persian Gulf War</u>.

1. Sad

2. Ray,

3. pepley a Sad

                                    There are no "right" or
                                    "wrong" answers.

4. pepe hope they come back

5. peple Wisaud cum back

Draw a picture that shows what you think or feel about the <u>Persian Gulf War</u>.

(Only use a pencil)

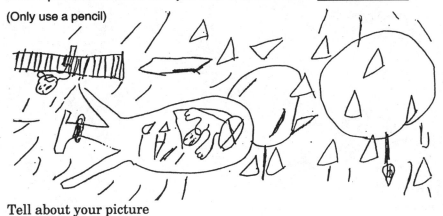

Tell about your picture

APPENDIX B (Cont'd.)

Name _____   Boy _____ Girl _✓_

Teacher _____

You have thoughts and feelings about the <u>Persian Gulf War</u>.

Write 5 words that come to mind when you think and feel about the <u>Persian Gulf War</u>.

1. Sad
2. scared
3. diying
4. bad
5. boms

There are no "right" or "wrong" answers.

Draw a picture that shows what you think or feel about the <u>Persian Gulf War</u>. (Only use a pencil)

Tell about your picture   The two lateys and the mon both diyed because of boms they shot down the plane and shot the lateys and Saidom Hasane is lagteing.

CHAPTER 8

AIDS and Our Children

Robert Fulton

Normally, as professional caregivers, we address a "problem" in terms of someone else. That is, it is someone else's illness or someone else's difficulty that commands our attention—not our own. In this chapter, however, I want to direct my remarks to you, concerning the AIDS epidemic, as parents and family members, in addition to your roles as men and women who are dedicated to the service of others. In the face of this burgeoning plague I think we are not only obligated to attend to those who are infected with HIV or who are afflicted with AIDS, but we must also acknowledge that—to varying degrees—we are all potentially at risk for this disease. To accept that fact has two advantages—or virtues—as it were. First, empathy is engendered. Through our ability to identify with others, we are encouraged to extend compassion toward those who have been stricken. Second, we are enjoined to confront the epidemic in our own homes and communities rather than exclusively in the isolated or segregated setting of the workplace, that is, the hospital or clinic. It is then that the epidemic becomes an immediate reality to one's self and family and thereby permits us to ask the personal questions and take the private actions that are necessary to forestall it. Also, we are empowered to ask: "What can I do as a parent, or as a member of my community, to alert others to the epidemic's implicit threat?" This chapter is my personal reply, as a parent and as a sociologist, to that question.

North American news media—television, radio, films, and newspapers—would have us believe that AIDS does not constitute a threat, at least not a significant one to our heterosexual, drug-free sons and daughters. The news media continue to characterize the epidemic—even after ten years—as essentially a scourge of homosexual men and

123

illicit drug-users (the so-called "socially-marginalized" groups). Categorically, they are wrong: Allow me to tell you why.

AIDS SURVEY

We recently conducted an AIDS survey of approximately 1000 first-year students at the University of Minnesota [1]. It enquired about their knowledge of the AIDS epidemic, as well as their social history and sexual behavior, both past and present. Because most white, middle-class parents believe that their children are not at risk for AIDS and because the media focus principally on minority members of the society when reporting the epidemic, we removed from the sample all minority students' responses: African-American, Asian, Hispanic, and Native American. The following is an overview of the 875 white students who participated freely and anonymously in the study.

Student Profile

Eight out of ten of the students were born and reared in Minnesota; their average age was twenty years. They came mostly from middle and upper middle-class homes in which at least one of the parents was professionally employed. The students reported an average family income of $62,000 a year. One-third of the students reported regular church attendance; altogether more than two-thirds indicated church participation of some kind. Denominationally, they were primarily Catholic and Lutheran. The students resided mainly in urban areas such as the Twin Cities of Minneapolis and St. Paul.

Sexual Behavior

What did the findings tell us about students' sexual behavior or their risk of contracting HIV? We already knew from a 1989 Board of Education state-wide health survey that six out of ten high school students engaged in sexual intercourse before graduation [2-3]. Our study served to confirm the Board's findings. It showed that, after the first year at university, eight out of ten students were sexually active. Simply stated, 80 percent of the students in our sample reported having had sexual intercourse (that is, vaginal or anal penetration) at least once, with at least one partner at the time of the study. Importantly, however, the study also showed that over half (54%) of the students, who disclosed being sexually active, had more than one lifetime sexual partner. The students reported an average of more than three partners each; the men reported ten, and the females reported seven, lifetime partners.

Disease Prevention

Of course we know that sexual activity, per se, does not automatically lead to venereal disease, let alone infection with HIV. Therefore, in order to determine students' risk of contracting a sexually-transmitted disease (STD), including the risk of HIV, we looked at their responses to the question dealing with disease prevention, specifically, the use of condoms. What we learned was that the students used condoms, generally, about half of the time. The study showed, for example, that 25 percent of those students who had a "single" partner "always" used a condom. On the other hand, students who indicated that they had "multiple" sex partners reported that they "always" used a condom less than 12 percent of the time. Importantly, for our discussion, almost one-third of both "multi-partner" and "single-partner" respondents revealed that they "never" used a condom.

But does failure to use a condom "every time" necessarily mean that students are at risk for a venereal disease? The answer to that question is problematic. It depends on the presence or absence of venereal diseases in the students' sexual network, that is, the group of men and women who are linked together because of their multiple, sexual relationships. Obviously, if a couple were monogamous and both free of disease there would be no risk—although there would be risk of pregnancy. On the other hand, if a young man or woman engages in "multi-partner" sex, and there is at least one venereal disease present in the sexual network, then a risk certainly exists, especially if no precautions are taken. Imagine a group of students, blind-folded, within a large enclosure. Imagine further that one student has red paint on his hands. Finally, imagine that, at certain intervals, each student reaches out and shakes the hand of three other students, sometimes with the same students and sometimes with different students. It would not be long before every student in the room had red paint on his or her hands. That is the analogous situation that young people face when they engage in multi-partner, unprotected sex in a semi-bounded institution like a college or university.

STDs On Campus

College campuses vary considerably with regard to the presence of venereal disease. Some campuses will report no cases while others will report that upwards of 15 percent of the students are infected with a STD. Research shows, however, an increasing prevalence of STDs on college campuses across the United States. Last year 600,000 new cases of chlamydia were recorded—the STD most often reported among adolescents and college students. What makes chlamydia so serious a disease for young women, in particular, is that it can remain asymptomatic for a long period of time or manifest mild and easily ignored symptoms. But chlamydia, like other venereal diseases: herpes, genital warts, gonorrhea, and syphilis, ruptures the epidermis or mucous membrane and thus allows direct access to the blood vascular system. Therefore, it can facilitate the transmission of HIV.

The students in our sample had a STD rate, on average, of 15 percent. However, the number of sexual partners was a critical determinant for risk of infection: students who reported one sexual partner had a STD rate of 6 percent while students who indicated two or more partners had a STD rate of 22 percent. Moreover, if a student came from a divorced or separated home and had "multi-partner" sexual relations, the STD rate was 31 percent. Later, I will address the important role that students from divorced homes played in the study. The "child of divorce" emerged as a critical figure in the survey and he/she must be discussed in detail.

When the analysis was extended further, it was found that students, who had sexual relations with more than one partner, were the least likely to use any kind of barrier protection against disease.

Preliminary Summary

What can we conclude from this brief review of the findings? Let me summarize: Of the 875 students in the sample, 80 percent were sexually active; more than half reported two or more lifetime sexual partners; one in five reported receiving treatment for a STD; and, if the respondent came from a divorced home, the STD rate was one in three. To this I must add that the students indicated—as they do on most other college campuses that have been surveyed—a competent level of knowledge about HIV and AIDS. The results of the survey that we administered showed that, overall, 84.5 percent of the students demonstrated a "superior" or "good" understanding of the epidemic.

What these few observations add up to, I believe, is the potential for an epidemic of HIV to occur among white, college-age men and women—an epidemic that will far surpass in numbers the calamity that has already occurred. I say this because the Center for Disease Control (CDC) in Atlanta has recently reported the presence of HIV on American college campuses. In a survey of nineteen institutions, both public and private, HIV was found to be present on nine campuses. While the over-all prevalance rate was relatively low—0.2 percent (2 per thousand), one campus revealed a prevalance rate of 1 percent.

In light of the evidence from the CDC and the fact that other STDs that are known to facilitate HIV infection are present on American campuses, we must face up to the reality of the epidemic and the threat that it presents to our children. The situation calls for an immediate and enlightened response from everyone: parents, administrators, and the students themselves. Not to act—not to raise an alarm—is to run the risk of having hundreds of thousands of young men and women exposed to HIV, perhaps dying a needless death. What I am talking about is unprecedented death, unprecedented loss, unprecedented grief in our time. We are not only looking at the loss, through death, of a sizeable portion of the next productive generation but we are also looking at the prospect of the reproductive generation being put at risk.

Children of Divorce

Permit me to return to the subject of divorce and the important role that young men and women from divorced homes may play—albeit inadvertently—in the AIDS epidemic. First allow me, however, to provide you with some necessary background information.

In 1973, I conducted a study on childhood bereavement with Robert Bendiksen, a graduate student [4]. We examined the social backgrounds of 11,000 ninth-grade students who, in 1956, participated in the pioneering research that served as the basis for the Minnesota Multi-phasic Personality Inventory (MMPI). Among that group of children were eight hundred boys and girls—about 7 percent of the total—whose parents had either been separated, divorced, or dead by the time of the study. The subjects, now in their early thirties, were contacted by way of a mailed questionnaire. Ten percent were also interviewed personally. What we found was that children who had come from homes broken by death responded to our questions in much the same way as children from "intact" families. Often, it was impossible to distinguish the behavioral characteristics and the reported social and emotional adjustments of those whose homes were "broken" by death and those who had come from an "intact" home. Time, social support, and the re-marriage of the parent(s) were reasons given for the recovery from loss. Those who were still having social or emotional problems of some kind, were not the respondents whose homes were shattered by a death, but rather, those who had come from homes "broken" by divorce. Problems still plagued them. They reported having problems with jobs, health, education, and authority—issues that were also problematic for them during their adolescent years. They described themselves as being "risk takers," especially with respect to the law. They not only reported more difficulties with authority than did the other two groups but they also reported this to be true of their siblings as well.

Because of the significance of these findings coupled with other research on the impact of divorce on children [5-10], I decided to examine separately the responses to the AIDS questionnaire by those students who had reported that their parents were divorced. The analysis showed that on every response, behavioral characteristic, social or sexual experience relevant to contracting a STD, students from "divorced" homes—as a group—were at higher "risk" than were students from "intact" homes. The study indicated, for instance, that children from "divorced" homes were more likely to be the first ones to be sexually active or to be exposed to the sexuality of others. The analysis showed that students from "divorced" homes were more likely to have read sexually explicit magazines, books, or viewed pornographic videotapes than students from "intact" homes. There was also more alcohol around; children from "divorced" homes would likely experiment with alcohol at an earlier age. They, moreover, experienced sex earlier—sometimes as early as elementary school. Childhood sexuality is a reality in America, as this study confirms. Finally, this study showed that children of divorce were, in all likelihood, the first to: experience sexual intercourse; experiment with drugs and alcohol; among women, get pregnant or have an abortion; and, for both men and women, be the first to contract a STD. In addition, as I have noted, they reported the highest rate of STDs (31.5%) of the different groups studied.

AIDS IN THE MEDIA

As parents, we must address this threat to the lives of our children in the most direct and forthright manner possible. How can we do that? First, I would suggest that neighborhood or community groups be formed to monitor the media in order to provide correct and undistorted information to the public, and particularly to children, about the epidemic. The media are perhaps most responsible for maintaining the fiction that AIDS is not a threat to the sexually-active, heterosexual population [11-13]. Let me provide you with an example of the way the epidemic has been, and continues to be, treated by the media in my own city of Minneapolis. Recently, there was a man who was a city supervisor. He was not only intelligent and eloquent but he also showed great concern for the poor and the underprivileged. As a result, he was greatly admired by a large sector of the population and was recognized as an important political figure. He was also gay. When he learned that he was HIV positive he informed the community of his sexual orientation and the status of his health. Much publicity surrounded this announcement. His picture was displayed in the newspapers and on television. Editorials were written about him extolling his honesty and courage. Ultimately, he died of AIDS. Hundreds of people attended his funeral which was considered important enough to be televised. Most of the political leaders of the city and state were present. Tremendous publicity surrounded his death and continued even after the funeral—front page and television reports—everything you can imagine. At the same time as media attention was being accorded to this gay man's death and funeral, there was, tucked away in the back pages of the Minneapolis newspaper, a report of twenty-six workers in a meat packing plant, in a small town in the southern part of the state, that were tested positive for HIV—this information was only back-page news. To the best of my knowledge the newspaper has, to this day, never followed through on the story—nor has any of the local television stations.

I would argue that the media, by their acts of commission and/or omission, help to perpetuate a "false consciousness" among American youth with respect to the epidemic and their degree of risk in relation to it. How many of you have heard yourself say, or heard others say, "Oh, young people think they are invulnerable, that is why they behave as they do and take such risks with their health and their lives?" Such a pronouncement makes it easy for us to wash our hands of any responsibility for their actions. But why should our children not feel invulnerable? Since the beginning of the epidemic, since they were only ten or eleven years of age, they have been informed by the media—and continue to be so informed—that their risk is remote. This is what the state-wide Board of Education, as well as our survey, showed. Furthermore, the Minnesota high school students reported that most of what they knew about the epidemic they had learned from the media or their friends—not from their teachers or parents. As a matter of fact, only one high school student in five reported receiving information from his or her parent(s) about sex, let alone about the AIDS epidemic. It is not just a matter of telling young people to "just say no." The Board of Education survey revealed that upward of 25 percent of the ninth-graders have already experienced sexual intercourse.

CONCLUSION

We are looking at an epidemic that is transmitted sexually. Our children are sexually active and in the face of the epidemic—recklessly so—but for reasons that are understandable. I believe that we, as parents, must do what we can to identify those reasons and eliminate them wherever possible. This means taking a personal responsibility to see that your child is correctly informed about the epidemic and that all sources of information for your child: church, school, media—and most importantly—your home, be committed to the task.

AFTERWORD

Since this study, the presence of HIV has been reported on the University of Minnesota campus.

REFERENCES

1. O. D. Weeks, M. P. Drew and R. Fulton, *AIDS on Campus? Knowledge of HIV and Risky Sexual Behavior of First-Year College Students,* unpublished manuscript, 1993.
2. Minnesota Department of Education, *Minnesota Student Survey Report 1989,* St. Paul, Minnesota, 1989.
3. Minnesota Department of Education, *Minnesota Student Survey: AIDS/HIV—Related Knowledge, Attitudes and Risk Behavior,* St. Paul, Minnesota, 1989.
4. R. Bendiksen and R. Fulton, Death and the Child: An Anterospective Test of the Childhood Bereavement and Later Behavior Disorder Hypothesis, in *Death and Identity* (Rev. Edition), R. Fulton and R. Bendiksen (eds.), Robert J. Brady Co., Bowie, Maryland, 1976.
5. J. Kunz, The Effects of Divorce on Children, in *Family Research: A Sixty-Year Review, 1930-1990,* Vol. 2, S. Bahr (ed.), Lexington Books, New York, pp. 325-376, 1991.
6. P.R. Amato and B. Keith, Parental Divorce and the Well-Being of Children: A Meta-Analysis, *Psychological Bulletin, 110*:1, pp. 26-46, 1991.
7. A. Z. Schwartzberg, The Impact of Divorce on Adolescents, *Hospital and Community Psychiatry, 43*:6, pp. 634-637, 1992.
8. D. S. Shaw, The Effects of Divorce on Children's Adjustment, *Behaviour Modification, 15*:4, pp. 456-485, 1991.
9. J. S. Wallerstein, The Long-Term Effects of Divorce on Children: A Review, *Journal of the American Academy of Child Adolescent Psychiatry, 30*:3, pp. 349-360, 1991.
10. I. L. Reiss, *The Social Context of Premarital Sexual Permissiveness,* Holt, Rinehart and Winston, Inc., New York, 1967.
11. A. M. Brandt, *No Magic Bullet: A Social History of Venereal Disease in the United States Since 1980,* Oxford University Press, New York, 1987.
12. Life, Picture of Two Men Portraying AIDS Compassion, *Life, 15*:1, p. 66, 1992.
13. Playboy Forum, Magic, *Playboy, 9*:3, pp. 41-45, 1992.

CHAPTER 9

Glimpses of the Impact of Childhood Cancer on the Child and Family in East Asia

Ida M. Martinson

Families who immigrate to another country may have children who develop cancer. As we are becoming more international, those of us who work with families who have children with cancer may benefit from information concerning selected portions of the world and what happens to those children and their families. An overview of several Asian countries and glimpses of their culture will begin this chapter and is followed by a brief review of the following questions:

- How does the culture influence the care provided?
- How do children deal with illness, pain and suffering?
- Who assists children with cancer and their families throughout the course of the illness from diagnosis to cure or death?[1]

INCIDENCE OF CHILDHOOD CANCER WORLDWIDE

Childhood cancers have a total incidence in most populations of only 100 to 150 cases per million children per year. According to the United Nations criterion for less developed countries, 129 countries account for

[1] Funding for the studies came from the National Science Council, Taipei, Taiwan, ROC, the National Academy of Sciences, Washington, D.C., the Fulbright Research Grant, St. Lukes Hospital School of Nursing, Tokyo, Japan, and the Department of Family Health Care Nursing.

77 percent of the world's population and 84 percent of the world's children are younger than the age of fifteen [1]. There are approximately 200,000 children who have cancer in the world with 70 percent living in the developing countries. When examining the improvements in treatment and the increased survival of children with cancer we need to consider the country's level of development in health care and the financial implications for the treatment of childhood cancer. We also need to examine the family's adjustment to childhood cancer and its impact on their lives. For instance, the overall average age for the onset of childhood cancer is five years and the treatment duration is from two to three years. Families must face the impact of the illness during child rearing years and deal with the strain of the illness on young siblings. Improved rates of survival and cure may extend the consequences of the illness for many years to come.

In this chapter, I will describe the impact of childhood cancer on children and their families in Taiwan, the Republic of China (ROC); China, the People's Republic of China (PRC); South Korea; and Japan. I will use the United States as a benchmark for contrast at various points. Although each study was conducted at different times within the past decade, my review will include comments which account for progress beyond the time of my original work.

BACKGROUND INFORMATION

Each year in the United States there are approximately 6,500 newly diagnosed children with cancer. Because of improved treatment regimens, over 60 percent of these children will be cured. It is estimated that, by the turn of the century, one out of every one thousand adults aged twenty will be a survivor of childhood cancer [2]. Although cancer is a relatively rare disease, it is the most common cause of disease-related deaths for children between the ages of two and sixteen [3]. In the United States, accidents cause the most deaths, while in many of the developing countries most deaths are caused by infectious diseases including diarrhea. However, as progress is made in the control of communicable diseases and diarrhea along with improvements in sanitation, childhood cancer will gradually become the most common cause of disease-related death in developing countries. Leukemia is the most common type of childhood cancer in the world today. It has been demonstrated in the United States that aggressive treatment of childhood cancer results in increased survival and long term retention of the quality of life for the child and family. If aggressive treatment programs can be implemented in developing countries, survival and cure rates should parallel those in the United States and other developed countries. Consequently, public education is essential so that children can be diagnosed early and treatment started immediately. The public needs to be aware that over 60 percent of children with cancer can be cured so that, where feasible, the resources for aggressive treatment can be implemented.

When treatment is unsuccessful the goal to maintain the quality of life for children who cannot be cured should be enhanced. Pediatric hospice care needs to be developed in most parts of the world. In addition, family education is vitally important so that family resources can be engaged to help children cope with the illness, treatment, and survival, or dying and death.

CULTURE

There are both overt and background issues that highlight the differences between cultures. For this chapter, I will comment on three categories of overt issues that directly affect families of children with cancer. These incorporate the material aspects, including the country's economy and technology; the symbolic aspects, encompassing cultural beliefs and religion; and the social dynamics, involving the network of obligations and responsibilities that affect decision-making in the family. Such issues are exemplified in the comparison of economic development, traditional understandings of health care and religious practices, and the structure of the family.

In my work it was apparent that each of the East Asian societies included a variation in the mix of traditional values and modern technological economic practices. On a scale from high to low, Japan clearly reflected the highest stage of economic and technological development, and China the lowest. China remained primarily a rural society while Japan was almost totally urbanized. At the time of the Taiwan study, in 1981, this country had only recently experienced the economic and social changes that accompany an urban centered society. Korea was already an established urban centered society when I conducted the study in 1990.

The scale differs when examining traditional and religious values. Here China reflected the greatest degree of secularization of values. Despite the resurgence of religion in much of China, traditional religions and their values were almost non-existent. Japan also reflected a strongly secularized value system despite the powerful presence of the new religions. Diffuse traditional values of Shinto, Confucian, and Buddhist provenance were in evidence while Christianity was a small, but not insignificant, presence. In Korea, traditional values were clearly evident, with the pervasive presence of

Confucian, Shammanist, and Buddhist values. But the strongest single religious presence was that of Christianity, making Korea the least traditional of the societies. As for Taiwan, the traditional values of folk religion, Confucianism and Buddhism were pervasive with Christianity remaining a small but significant presence.

In respect to health care, China was the most traditional with its highly integrated system of traditional Chinese medicine with Western medicine. Both could be easily obtained in hospitals or clinics as needed or desired by the family. In Taiwan, there were clear distinctions between Western and Chinese medicine. Traditional Chinese herbs were readily available from within their own set of clinics, whereas western medicine was the main stay of most government clinics and hospitals. However, a third component of the health care delivery system existed in the temples where priests and fortune tellers were consulted for diagnosis and treatment. In Korea, traditional herbs and treatment were available only to patients who knew where to obtain them.

Further variance in the characteristics of the countries were apparent in respect to family structures. Taiwan, in the early 1980s, retained remnants of the traditional extended family which once dominated rural areas. But this pattern was gradually being broken with the move toward an urban-industrial society and the dominance of the nuclear family. China reflected a different pattern which was influenced, no doubt, by its communist history. China remained an overwhelmingly rural society, but one in which the extended family no longer seemed to function effectively. Fragmentation of the rural society into nuclear families was the dominant pattern. Korea, being a well developed urban culture, also showed a dominance of the nuclear family. The sense of hierarchy in the family seemed the strongest, and a sense of responsibility to the older generation was the least attenuated of these societies. Japan was the most highly urbanized society. Nuclear families predominated, but a well developed sense of responsibility for the older generation remained.

TAIWAN, ROC

First let us look at Taiwan, ROC, a beautiful island located south of Japan and one hundred miles west of southern China. In 1990, its population was thirty million including seven million children. In 1978, the overall death rate for children was 6.5 per 100,000 versus 4.7 per 100,000 in the United States. In 1981, we also examined why the death rate for children with cancer was greater and questioned if the traditional large extended Chinese family offered parents and children a helpful network of emotional and social support. It was clear that no other studies had examined these issues. Consequently, a cross sectional research design was utilized to study the following families intensively: twenty-five families of newly diagnosed children, twenty-five families in which children were not expected to live because of uncontrollable cancer, and twenty-five families in which children had already died from cancer. In-depth interviews included the parents, children with cancer who were over five years of age, available siblings, and grandparents. One of the major findings indicated that one out of three families were in debt because of the cost of treating childhood cancer [4]. At that time, there was no health insurance to cover the costs and families were required to pay in advance for both hospitalization and medications. As a result, some parents could not afford to treat their children. As one sibling, whose brother died from cancer, said to the interviewer, "I would commit suicide if I had cancer because my brother had too much pain and the costs to the family are unbearable, my own children will still need to repay the debt we have." Another mother told us of her wish to buy enough sleeping medication to put her dying child out of the misery of the pain and then she would kill herself. Situations such as these convinced the research team that action was needed to help families of children with cancer in Taiwan.

In 1982, the development of the Childhood Cancer Foundation resulted in extensive contributions of funds that enabled children with cancer to receive the necessary chemotherapy for the two or three years of required treatment. The number of children dying from cancer was reduced from 406 in 1978 to 300 in 1991, while the number of children being treated for cancer increased during this time. Pediatric oncologists have joined together in clinical trials that enable children in any part of the island to receive the same treatment. As a result, it is no longer necessary for children to make the long trip to large treatment centers. In addition, nurses have received an intensive program in pediatric oncology nursing. More than twenty nurses have attended two weeks of on-site training in the United States to become clinical specialists in pediatric oncology.

As well as supporting both of the above, the Childhood Cancer Foundation has developed education materials for families of children with cancer. These include pamphlets on nutrition, indwelling catheters, radiotherapy, and specific disease information booklets on leukemia, lymphoma, retinoblastoma, bone tumors, brain tumors, and Wilm's tumor. In addition, parent group meetings and gatherings for children take place throughout the year. Major progress has been made in the treatment of childhood cancer and ongoing support programs have been developed. Emphasis has been given to pain control. Plans for hospice care for children are being initiated. More than 2,000 families have received assistance from the foundation [5, 6].

Cultural Illustration

The influence of culture was illustrated most clearly in the extended family and the religious response of the families at diagnosis, during treatment of cancer, and in death rituals if the children died [7]. Some families sought out advice and guidance from the temples even in such matters as surgery for their children. In one family, after the grandfather had inquired at the temple whether his grandson should have surgery for the removal of a Wilm's tumor, the child was taken home without the necessary surgery. Within a year, as the child became increasingly ill, a fortune teller finally encouraged the grandfather to allow the surgery, however, the operation was no longer possible and the child died. In other families, the religious activities provided emotional support during the long period of aggressive treatment.

How Children Dealt with their Illness and Treatment

In Taiwan, children with cancer frequently knew they had cancer and struggled with pain during treatments and terminal care. Since 1981, there have been major improvements in pain control because children may now receive morphine. It was revealing to ask these children to describe their three wishes. Their responses provided valuable insights into their experience with cancer and what they hoped and dreamed for [8]. Children, as they became older, more frequently expressed the wish to get well. One adolescent revealed his first wish was "not to die so soon."

Assistance to the Child and Family

As in many countries, parents in Taiwan are the major source of support and assistance to children with cancer. Health care providers need to be more alert to the many demands placed on parents and families [9]. Attention also needs to be given to siblings to help them adapt to the changes in their lives [10]. Caregivers can provide assistance by taking more time to be with the children, listening to them, answering their questions, and being available to address their concerns. Through its programs, the Childhood Cancer Foundation has improved the care of children with cancer and spearheaded major improvements in their survival.

CHINA, PRC

Since one out of five people in the world are Chinese; it can be estimated that, at least one out of every ten children with cancer are Chinese. In 1989, a major study on the impact of childhood cancer on families in China was conducted at Sun Yat-Sen University of Health Sciences in Guangzhou in the southern province of Guangdung [11]. Close to fifty million people live in the province of Guangdung. Children with cancer from throughout the province are treated at one of the hospitals affiliated with Sun Yat-Sen University of Health Sciences.

The cost of treating a child with cancer in China is approximately 1,500 RMB per month, while the salary of a rural farmer is only 500 RMB per year. The average salary of a teacher is from 120 to 200 RMB per month. The wealthiest family involved in the study earned 800 RMB per month. All families who had to completely pay for the treatment and hospitalization of their children were experiencing major financial difficulties. They expressed grave concern about the possibility of not being able to continue the treatment for the full length of time needed to offer the best potential of cure for their children [12].

At the end of 1992, the Amity Foundation in Nanjing adopted the Childhood Cancer Project. Funds are being sought from within China and worldwide so that children with cancer can receive the necessary medical care. In addition, the Childhood Cancer Foundation of Taiwan generously permitted translation of their educational materials for use in the PRC and Project Hope funded the translation costs. These materials are now in use in parts of China. At present, families continue to do their best to provide for their children's medical treatment, even when it depletes all of their financial resources.

Cultural Illustration

Confucian influences on families and the political upheavals of recent times may have increased the lack of contact and support between families. People have been encouraged to recognize that others have all that they can manage and should be left alone. Consequently, families of children with cancer are expected to keep to themselves. We noted that parents often remained in hospital with their child for many months without any involvement from other parents. Since there were no parent group meetings or discussions, parents were left on their own to cope with their children.

How Children Dealt with their Illness and Treatment

Children with cancer were frequently hospitalized for months at a time for the following reasons:

- children lived too far away from any competent health care team that included a pediatric oncologist
- the hospital was the major center for the provision of medications
- remaining in hospital as long as possible offered the best chance of recovery.

During their stay it was evident that most children knew they had cancer. Usually their mother or father was present at all times in order to provide emotional support, prepare food, and assist with routine care. When asked about their three wishes all children wished to recover and go home. Younger children wanted special foods to eat, while older children hoped for funds so their families would have enough money to maintain regular living. Children also wished to attend school, play, and be cured. Older children and adolescents requested more information about their illness and treatment. Many expressed the hope that they would recover rather than die. Their awareness is reflected in the case of an eleven-year-old boy who knew he was going to die. This boy wanted to comfort his younger brother so he would not feel bad when he died. In another situation, an adolescent girl with a guarded prognosis was being treated for leukemia. She was anxious because she knew that if her treatment continued her parents would totally exhaust their financial resources and she might still die. It was common for Chinese families to struggle and to borrow the funds necessary for treatment.

Assistance to the Child and Family

Clearly, funds are needed to provide the essential medical treatment to cure children with cancer and to provide long-term quality of life to others. In Tianjin, with the support of a nursing professor who used the basic components of pediatric hospice care practices, two children with cancer have died at home. In our study, it was clear that caregivers needed to spend more time listening to the concerns of children and families. It was also apparent that pain control was not achieved for most children with cancer. In the future, when the WHO (World Health Organization) Guidelines for Control of Pediatric Oncology Pain and for Palliative Care are released, it is hoped that these will provide the stimulus for the health system to address the needs for pain control.

SOUTH KOREA

South Korea is east of Northern China and west of Japan. It has a population of forty-two million, eleven million of which are children under the age of fifteen. In 1988, according to government statistics, 712 children were diagnosed with cancer and 605 children had died from cancer. In South Korea, the health care insurance policy includes the treatment of childhood cancer for eight months out of every year. There are plans to expand this health care insurance policy to cover treatment of childhood cancer for all twelve months of the year. Two voluntary organizations already exist which assist Korean families with the costs of treatment. The Korean Heart Association provides the funds for bone marrow transplantation and the Korean Social Welfare Program provides families with the necessary funds so that children with cancer, regardless of their economic level, are able to continue and complete their treatment.

Cultural Illustration

Over one-third of the country is Christian. Churches are very active in providing support to families in need. At night lighted crosses are everywhere. In our study, families identified religious beliefs as a positive influence. One family with a newly diagnosed child had joined the church and been baptized with the hope of receiving a cure for their child. They had moved from the southern part of Korea to Seoul to be near the treatment center. The mother was very concerned that she may have fed the child something that had caused the cancer. This concern was associated with the fact that mothers are frequently held responsible for their child's illness by the older members of the extended family.

How Children Dealt with their Illness and Treatment

In most instances, children in our study knew that they had cancer but did not fully comprehend the consequences. Although some comfort measures for pain were used, pain control was a major problem. It was difficult for both mothers and children when children were in pain because the mothers were the primary caregivers both in the hospital and at home. In one situation, a six-year-old boy developed abdominal pains which his mother believed were a result of not digesting his food properly. She treated him with Korean folk medicine and was advised by a local clinic that he had a minor ailment. Finally, when the pain persisted, the parents went to the Children's Hospital where the child was diagnosed with a malignant late-stage sarcoma. Two operations later, the situation was hopeless and his death was inevitable.

As in other cultures, when children's hair fell out due to treatment, other children laughed. The children whose hair had fallen out told the researchers that they felt very sad.

Assistance to the Child and Family

In South Korea, the major problems for families included spousal conflicts, negative responses from siblings, separation of the family members due to long hospitalizations, and economic hardships due to the high cost of long term medical and hospital care [13, 14]. Since parents depended on each other for emotional support during what was often a protracted illness, marital distress was especially taxing. When children died, family members often described a feeling of emptiness. This was accompanied by sadness, emotional pain, and bitterness resulting in changes in attitudes about life, modification of religious practices, changes in family relationships, and difficulties with personal health [15].

It was clear that caregivers can be most helpful when they listen to children and their families and are willing to answer the many questions that arise during the process of cancer treatment. Both home and hospice care are needed to provide these families with comprehensive care.

JAPAN

In 1990, Japan was composed of approximately 120 million people residing on several islands in the Pacific. Japan was the first non-Western country to develop universal social insurance plans for all citizens, including children. Under these plans parents must pay 20 percent of inpatient and 30 percent of outpatient health care costs for their children. As a result, childhood cancer families are required to pay up to a maximum of $400 U.S. per month [16]. Since 1978, there has been an active Japanese Association for Childhood Cancer that has made coverage of childhood cancer treatment possible for all families in Japan. At present, even with advances and availability of aggressive medical treatment, approximately 750 children die from childhood cancer each year.

Cultural Illustration

Japanese culture is rooted in the ancient Shinto tradition in which divinity (kami) is embedded within the structures of society, including the family, thereby contributing to its long term stability and cohesiveness. However Japan, like Korea, also has been profoundly shaped by the Confucian ethos which is derived from China. Basic to this ethos is the central role of the family which, as the model for society as a whole, is structured in an essentially hierarchical manner. The priority of the male head of the family lies above all in his moral authority and this is expressed socially through the obedience of the wife and the filial attitude of the children toward the father. Religious confirmation is received in the male-dominated ancestral rites. Also, Japan has been profoundly shaped by Buddhism. Unlike China and Korea, the ancestral rites in Japan have been largely integrated into the Buddhist rites for the dead. Accordingly, it is not possible to understand the Japanese family without reference to all three of these traditions at the same time.

Some years ago I experienced a dramatic confirmation of these complex traditions. I was intrigued by the small statues of children, usually with a cap on the head and a bib around the neck, arranged in serried ranks often by the hundreds on Buddhist temple grounds. My inquiries revealed that these were placed in ritual remembrance of aborted fetuses.

A complex overlapping of traditions exists in which the Shinto sense of a divine quality adhering to the living, as well as to the spirits of the dead, is overlaid by a Confucian sense of the moral community of the living with the dead. This, in turn, is given further depth in a Buddhist rite which seeks to give a good rebirth to the unfortunate dead. This complex ethos has profound implications on how the Japanese family responds to the traumas of childhood cancer.

How Children Dealt with their Illness and Treatment

Children with cancer usually remained in hospital for extended periods. Mothers stayed with them at all times while a grandmother assumed the care of the other children at home. Children were not told about the seriousness of their disease or its name and discussions with children about the illness and treatment were very limited. One informative mother said, "I told my daughter everything because I wanted her to understand why she had to receive painful treatments. However, I did not use the word *cancer*" [17].

It was common for parents to be upset when children asked questions about their illness. One˙Japanese girl asked her mother what death was like. When her parents asked the physician how they should respond, he initially suggested that the child talk with her grandparents since they were closer to death. Though the grandparents refused to talk to their granddaughter, she continued to inquire about death. The parents again returned to the physician for help. This time, he referred them to the hospital chaplain who met with the child several times. She was fascinated by the angel in the hospital chapel and asked to be baptized before she died. This experience had a uniting effect on the family because the parents were also baptized with their child.

Assistance to the Child and Family

In Japan, the mother is the primary caregiver for the sick child. Health care professionals need to be prepared to help mothers gain support from family members. Where feasible, they also need help to recognize when and how to meet the needs of their other children. From the time of diagnosis and throughout the child's illness, parent support groups can be very helpful to these Japanese families. Follow up for the families after the death of a child from cancer is worth pursuing.

CONCLUSION

Financially, the child with cancer in the United States, Japan, and Taiwan have the best chance of being cured without a complete financial collapse for the family. South Korea is moving toward full financial coverage for childhood cancer treatment, while China has the longest way to go.

In both South Korea and Japan, mothers provide most of the caregiving and are often held responsible for not protecting their children from developing cancer. In contrast, fathers in Taiwan participate more actively in the care of their children. In China, fathers in rural areas frequently accompany their ill children and remain with them during hospitalization and treatment.

It was obvious in our studies that most school-aged children knew about their disease despite attempts by family members and health care professionals to keep this information from them. It was clear that children were ready and eager to share their wishes. Younger children more frequently desired toys or special foods, while older children wanted to be cured, to go to school, and to avoid death.

It is clear that in Taiwan, China, South Korea, and Japan there is new hope that the availability of current treatment methods will be available throughout these countries. However, health care providers in all countries, including the United States, must continue to deal with the reality that some children will not survive. For dying children, services in some countries are also improving. For example, hospice care in the United States is gradually becoming available in many areas. In contrast, Japan has no known pediatric hospices at this time and families frequently take their children home to die. In 1992, the Oun On Foundation funded the development of a pediatric hospice demonstration model for South Korea. Taiwan has begun a hospice movement which will include children dying from cancer.

ACKNOWLEDGMENTS

Appreciation is expressed to the families and children with cancer who participated in these studies. Acknowledgment is given to Dr. Paul Martinson for his contribution to the materials in the sections dealing with cultural aspects.

REFERENCES

1. D. Parrin, C. Siller, G. Draper, and C. Bieber, The International Incidence of Childhood Cancer, *International Journal on Cancer, 42*, pp. 511-522, 1988.
2. A. Meadows and W. Hobbie, The Medical Consequences of Cure, *Cancer, 58*, pp. 524-528, 1986.
3. J. L. Young, L. G. Ries, E. Silverber, J. W. Horm, and R. W. Miller, Cancer Incidence, Survival and Mortality for Children Younger than Age 15 Years, *Cancer, 58*, pp. 598-602, 1986.
4. I. M. Martinson, Y. C. Chen, B. Y. Liu, L. H. Lo, J. C. Ou, R. H. Wang, and Y. M. Chao, Impact of Childhood Cancer on the Chinese Families, *Medical Science, 4*:4, pp. 1395-1415, 1982.
5. Y. C. Chen, Y. M. Chao, I. M. Martinson, Y. Lai, B. Kao, and G. Tseng, The Impact of Childhood Cancer on the Chinese Family—A Ten Year Follow-Up Study, *35th Anniversary of National Taiwan University's School of Nursing Research Report*, pp. 89-104, 1991.
6. I. M. Martinson, Impact of Childhood Cancer on Family Care in Taiwan, *Pediatric Nursing, 15*:6, pp. 636-637, 1989.
7. P. V. Martinson and I. M. Martinson, The Religious Response of the Chinese Family to Childhood Cancer, *American Asian Review, 6*:3, pp. 59-92, 1988.
8. I. M. Martinson and B. Y. Liu, Three Wishes of a Child with Cancer, *International Nursing Review, 35*:5, pp. 143-146, 1988.

9. Y. C. Chen, Y. M. Chao, and I. M. Martinson, An Analysis of Parents' Reaction to Childhood Cancer, in *Recent Advances in Nursing Series: Caring for Sick Children*, C. Barnes (ed.), Churchill Livingstone, London, England, pp. 61-84, 1987.
10. R. H. Wang and I. M. Martinson, A Study of the Impact of the Child with Cancer on Siblings in Chinese Family, *The NAROC Journal of Nursing, 29*, pp. 81-91, 1982.
11. I. M. Martinson and Y. H. Liang, The Reaction of Chinese Children who have Cancer, *Pediatric Nursing, 18*:4, pp. 345-349, 1993.
12. I. M. Martinson, S. X. Yin, and Y. H. Liang, The Impact of Childhood Cancer on Fifty Chinese Families, *Journal of Pediatric Oncology Nursing, 10*:1, pp. 13-18, 1993.
13. Y. Cho, S. Kim, and I. M. Martinson, The Experience of Families of Children being treated for Cancer: Sharing the Pain, *Nursing Science, 4*, pp. 17-29, 1992.
14. S. Kim, I. M. Martinson and S. Yang, The Impact of Childhood Cancer on the Korean Family, *Korean Academic Society of Nursing, 15*:4, pp. 495-511, 1992.
15. S. Yang, I. M. Martinson, and S. Kim, Qualitative Study on Experiences of Parents whose Child is Dying with Cancer, *Korean Academic Society of Nursing, 22*:4, pp. 512-526, 1992.
16. N. Ikegami, Japan: Maintaining Equity Through Regulated Fees, *Journal of Health Politics, Policy and Law, 17*:4, pp. 689-713, 1992.
17. S. Saiki, I. M. Martinson, and M. Inano, Japanese Families who have lost Children to Cancer: Primary Study, *Journal of Pediatric Nursing, 9*:4, pp. 239-250, 1994.

CHAPTER 10

The Renewal of Ritualization: Funerals of the 1990s

O. Duane Weeks

WHY CHILDREN NEED RITUAL

A sense of independence is often touted as a beneficial ingredient for personal, business and financial success. Independence carried to an extreme, however, can be harmful when considered in terms of social development.

American society began as a form of independence, a break from the past. Early settlers came to America in an attempt to free themselves from religious or government persecution. The westward movement was accomplished by courageous pioneers who wanted the chance to succeed or experience more individual freedom. Both the settlers and pioneers achieved the greater individual freedom that they sought, but their achievement was at the expense of separation from family and friends who were left behind. Like rebellious teenagers, Americans generally have always been enticed by the appeal of greener pastures, the chances they had to explore further, build bigger, earn more, and achieve greater goals than either their ancestors in foreign lands or their immediate predecessors.

The present generation of young Americans, it would appear, has now expanded the break with their heritage. Many young people do not see the past as a source of helpful tradition, values, or skills. Instead, they view the past as outdated, useless, and something to be ignored.

Not only are young people ignoring the past, they are also unsure of the future. The threat of nuclear annihilation, the menace of global warming, the starvation in Africa, the AIDS epidemic, the natural disasters such as floods and earthquakes, the serial killings, and the random drive-by shootings have created a catastrophic and fatalistic mentality. This mentality casts doubts on whether or not there will be a future and, if there is, will it be worthwhile?

In addition to their distrust of the past and uncertainty about the future, young people have an over-developed sense of independence because of the disintegration of the traditional family. The rate and number of divorces in the United States has increased from 385,000 (2.6 per 1,000 population) in 1950 to 1,189,000 (5.2 per 1,000) in 1980, and to 1,175,000 (4.7 per 1,000) in 1990 [1]. Since 1972, each year over 1,000,000 children have experienced the divorce of their parents. Bumpass has estimated that 41 percent of American children born to married women have their parents' marriage disrupted by separation, divorce, or death before they reach the age of sixteen [2].

The impact of divorce on children must not be underestimated. There are those instances, such as child abuse, in which divorce is necessary for the mental and physical well-being of the children. Most of the time, however, children suffer long-term negative consequences when their parents divorce. Many studies have demonstrated that children of divorce face greater social and emotional difficulties during childhood and adolescence than do children from maritally intact homes [3-8].

When we consider the effects of their distrust of the past, their uncertainty about the future, and their sense of insecurity caused by the disintegration of the traditional family, it becomes apparent that many young people are paying for their sense of independence by living, in effect, in a vacuum. They are separated from, and unaffected by, their environment. Therefore, it seems essential to reduce the vacuum effect of independence by forming bonds between young people and their social surroundings, including their family, their past, and their future. One way to form attachments between people and their social surroundings is through the use of rituals.

THE IMPORTANCE OF RITUALS

Rituals provide us with ties to others. The Christian ritual of Holy Baptism is used to bind the baptized person to Christ and to fellow believers. Bar mizvah is a ritual celebrated in Judaism where a boy is recognized as having attained the age of responsibility and religious duty. In many cultures, the ritual of marriage forms an outward bond between two partners. Rituals are used in fraternal organizations to make the members feel more closely akin to one another and to separate themselves from outsiders.

Funeral rituals serve a slightly different purpose. While they bind us to other mourners in our common grief, they also formally facilitate our separation from the person who has died. Somewhat analogous to graduation ceremonies, funeral rituals are, at the same time, rituals of binding and release.

Whether a death is of a grandparent, parent, spouse, lover, friend, or acquaintance, there is a change, a sense of loss, and a feeling of emptiness that cannot easily be relieved without the ties provided by funeral rituals. Funeral rituals facilitate social support for the family of the one who has died, as well as providing the community with an opportunity to recognize and externalize its sense of loss. Both Sanders and Rando have explained the purposes of death rituals as a means ". . . to separate the living from the dead, to provide the survivors with impetus to continue their lives . . ." [9, p. 96] while such rituals also ". . . catalyze acute grief responses, prescribe structural behaviors in time of flux, and encourage recognition of the loss and development of new relationships with both the deceased and community" [10, p. 190]. It is only necessary to recall the elaborate rituals surrounding the death and burial of President Kennedy to understand the perceptions of healing and continuity that rituals provide.

Whether toddlers, preschoolers, pre-teens, or adolescents, children need to feel that same support, healing, and continuity. Their sense of independence must be contained within a social comfort zone that can be provided by death and funeral rituals. An example of the value of death rituals may be found by comparing the values of such rituals with the values of gang membership. The decline of membership in social organizations such as the Masonic and Odd Fellows Lodges indicates that the present generation of young adults has little interest in ritualistic organizations based on historic values. The increase in membership of youth gangs, however, may indicate a continued need of young people to be involved in some sort of social organization. Gangs are based on the present, are self-serving, protective, and tend to alienate their members from the larger society. Thus, gang members will withdraw from society and neglect their social responsibility.

However, children who understand and participate in rituals of the larger social order will derive a sense of societal progression, with an appreciation for the past, a responsibility for the present, and a commitment to the future. Death rituals and other social rituals provide a means of attaching young people to their families and to their wider circle of social and cultural environments, thus decreasing their sense of isolation and selfishness while increasing their awareness of social affiliation and individual and collective responsibility.

Although there has been a movement in recent years toward more personalized funeral ceremonies, current funerals are still too often characterized by monochromatic liturgical prayers and hymns, with little to honor the individual characteristics of the person who died or provide comfort for the mourners. To be beneficial to anyone, and especially to children, funeral ceremonies must have meaning, and to have meaning, ceremonies must be personal.

This chapter provides a brief review of some historic death rituals, followed by a comparison of how children were affected by death and death rituals in the twentieth century, and how they are affected now. It will lead to a proposed return to helpful rituals in funerals of the 1990s and will conclude with specific suggestions for personalizing funeral services for children.

HISTORIC DEATH RITUALS

Before such events were recorded, perhaps since the beginning of human society, rituals and ceremonies were practiced at the time of death. Archaeologists have found evidence of shells, pottery, implements, and other material objects that were buried with the dead more than 50,000 years ago. The placing of these material objects, along with body preparations, indicates a concern for the afterlife of the dead as well as an attempt to formalize the relationship between the dead and those remaining alive [11]. In short, these were ritualistic acts that comforted the survivors.

Like the Neanderthal burials thousands of years earlier, it was a practice in ancient Egyptian society to carefully prepare the bodies of all who died—from royalty and wealth to the poorer classes—as well as providing material possessions so the dead could endure a journey of great length before a reunion of soul and preserved body in the afterlife [12].

The importance of proper burial ritual is emphasized in the Hebrew Bible where Abraham requested a burial site for his wife Sarah: "I am an alien and a stranger among you. Sell me some property for a burial site here so I can bury my dead" [13, p. 26]. Another Hebrew writer, identified as the preacher, reiterated Abraham's concern when he taught that:

> A man may have a hundred children and live many years; yet no matter how long he lives, if he cannot enjoy his prosperity and does not receive proper burial, I say that a stillborn child is better off than he [14, p. 871].

In North America, Native American burial practices varied according to the region, the tribe, and the historical setting. In the midwestern United States and the plains territories of Canada, one common practice was to wrap the dead in a blanket and place the blanketed body on a wooden scaffold erected above the plains. Another practice, noted in southern Alberta, was the burial of a dead brave with his worldly possessions, including his still living wife.

Neanderthal, Egyptian, Hebrew, and Native American burial customs all serve to illustrate the continuing importance of ritual in different cultures at different times.

1900 - 1990

Perhaps the clearest way to illustrate the differences between how children were affected by death in the early 1900s versus the 1990s is by comparing fictitious children living in the midwestern United States in 1900 with fictitious children living there in 1990.

In 1900, many families of the Midwest were extended families, that is, several generations of the same family lived on one farm. When a son of the original farm owner grew to adulthood, he often courted, married, and brought his bride to live in the farmhouse with his parents. The new couple had children, continued to live and work on the farm, and thus three generations of the same family lived together. When the grandfather, for example, became ill, he stayed on the farm and was cared for by his extended family, including the grandchildren. They would visit with him, read to him, run errands for him, and, when necessary, feed him. They were with him during his illness and, when he died, they were involved in the death experience. Women in the neighborhood along with women in the family, including granddaughters, were expected to clean and dress the body, arrange the parlor for visitation, and generally prepare for visitors. Neighbor men and men in the family, including grandsons, were expected to make the coffin, put the body in the coffin, carry the coffin to the country church, dig the grave, bury the coffin, and fill in the grave. Both women and men attended the funeral service.

In 1900, children also experienced the deaths of their siblings and, whenever death occurred in the family, it was considered part of the life cycle. For children in 1900, death was part of their natural experience and obligations to the dying and dead were considered sacred.

In the 1990s, there are only approximately one-third the number of American farms as compared to the number in 1900 [15]. Among those children who are still raised on farms, many move to metropolitan areas as soon as they are old enough to consider themselves independent. If children want to farm the family property, their parents usually move to a nearby small town and retire, or sometimes live in town and provide occasional part-time help on the farm. Thus, the farm family is nuclear. An extended farm family is a rarity since most children are now reared in an urban or suburban environment, and those families who do remain on a farm are nuclear rather than extended.

When the grandfather of the 1990s children becomes ill, he is usually taken to a hospital where visitation by children is not encouraged. Prolonged illness results in admission to a nursing home where he is seldom visited by his grandchildren. Professional nursing care substitutes for extended family visits, participation in providing individual care, and attention to the grandfather. This is not to say that the nursing care is not loving and personal. But it is not the loving and personal care provided by the grandchildren, and so they do not benefit from the unique experiences and interactions with their dying grandfather. When the grandfather dies ("expires" in medical terminology), his family is notified by telephone, and his body is entrusted to the care of the funeral director, another professional who prepares the body either for burial or cremation. There may or may not be a funeral service, the children are sometimes not allowed to see the body, and the process of death is quietly, if not secretly, concluded. For 1990s children, the death of their grandfather is impersonal and unnatural. It is a foreign process from which they are excluded, often by "protective" parents who are afraid of exhibiting or observing emotion. Children see death as an ending, outside of the life cycle. The secrecy and denial of death that surround children leaves them feeling that death is profane, rather than sacred.

AVOIDANCE OF FUNERALS

Children and adolescents tend to perceive themselves as immortal. They have seen dozens, hundreds, perhaps thousands of instances of death reported on television news, portrayed on television movies or dramas, or dramatically magnified on the plethora of "investigative" network programs that defile objective standards of conscientious news reporting. They have seen the deaths of others so often that they believe death happens to someone else, not to them. When one of their peers dies or is killed, it is because he or she "was stupid" or "had bad luck," and therefore, death "could never happen to me."

Not only has the media caused American youth to perceive themselves as immortal, but youth tend to be fixed on the present [16]. They conceive of death as an "event" that happens to the elderly

[17]. Therefore, they believe, when and if their own death occurs, they will have lived a full and long life. This unreal sense of personal immortality, their fixation on the present, and their conception of death as an "elderly" event make it difficult for children to personalize death [11]. Thus, it is to be expected that adolescents and young adults in America will attempt to avoid death and funerals, continuing to delude themselves into thinking that death only happens to others.

Even when children choose to attend a funeral, parents often erroneously believe that their children can be better protected if they are not allowed to attend. Thus, shunning funerals, whether voluntarily or involuntarily, is one way for children to avoid facing their own mortality. In addition, the lack of participation in funerals and other death rituals may result in a separation from the community of mourners and an inability to grieve constructively. Therefore, in reality, the effort of avoiding funerals becomes a harmful rather than a helpful exercise. My favorite tombstone inscription is:

> Remember friend, as you pass by,
> As you are now, so once was I,
> As I am now, so you shall be, so
> prepare yourself to follow me.
> — Anonymous

This epitaph eloquently illustrates the dilemma faced by American youth when they consider whether or not to attend a funeral. They may want to attend the service, extend or receive support, and share in the collective grief, but to do so would be to confront their own personal mortality. In addition, children, and especially adolescents, want to maintain an image of toughness and independence. Their participation in funeral services may precipitate an unwelcome show of emotion or inadequacy, and that would be incompatible with their desired image. Teenagers often express their fear of "breaking down" during a funeral service. Frequent comments include, "I don't want to cry," "Funerals make me sad," or "What can I possibly say?"

Children of all ages should be encouraged to attend funerals. Their attendance provides support and a sense of community and family continuity. Such involvement increases their social ties to family and community, provides them with a personal sense of belonging, and validates and supports their own grief work. It is only through meaningful ritual that these benefits can be accomplished.

HOW TO RETURN TO RITUAL

Children and adults can return to ritual and personalize funerals. I know many funeral directors, clergy, and counselors who are encouraging families to avoid surrogate sufferers and increase family participation in funeral rituals.

Surrogate sufferers are those who, usually with good intentions, take over duties that are, and should be, the responsibility of the nearest survivor. By assuming these duties, surrogate sufferers believe that they are relieving the trauma of the nearest survivor. They are, in effect, only delaying and increasing the trauma. Thus, surrogate sufferers—for example, the clergy person who offers to make all arrangements for the services; the sons who insist on going to make funeral arrangements at the funeral home office in place of their mother; and the funeral director who offers to complete all arrangement details—act as barriers that impede the work of immediate survivors in reconciling their grief. Worden has identified four tasks of mourning that need to be completed by the person who is bereft [18]. These tasks can be accomplished more expeditiously without the interference of surrogate sufferers.

SPECIFIC TASKS

If families, including children, are to avoid surrogate sufferers and increase family participation in death rituals, there are some specific tasks that will facilitate this involvement. Some families are able and willing to do more than others, and it is important not to force anyone to participate to the point of discomfort. Carlson, for example, has suggested that families can provide complete care for a member who has died [19]. Most family members may find that degree of responsibility too difficult. However, the following tasks may assist families to achieve maximum participation, including, but not limited to, children's involvement.

Making Funeral Arrangements

As many family members as possible should personally take part in making the funeral arrangements. Decisions should be made jointly concerning the service format; choice of the officiant; selection of music and musicians; and preference for memorial books, acknowledgment cards, and memorial folders. Collective decisions should be made regarding disposition of the body; choice of a cemetery or other place of internment; and, if a casket is used, the casket bearers. Including children in these arrangements provides them with a sense of belonging rather than feeling abandoned at a time when something major is happening in the family.

Contacting Ceremony Participants

Family members, including children, should contact and invite people to participate in the funeral ceremony. Tasks such as requesting help from the casket bearers, discussing musical selections with the musicians, or detailing the deceased person's life with a clergy person, enable family members to express and purge their feelings regarding the death; allow them to personally receive condolences; evoke memories of their lives with the person who has died; personalize the relationship between those involved in the ceremony and family members; and assist ceremony participants in making the funeral service more personal for the mourners.

Grooming the Body

Children, usually those who are older, may wish to assist in grooming or preparing the body of a parent, grandparent, or sibling. They may want to dress the body, arrange the hair, or help lift the body into the casket.

During the Visitation

Parents often determine that their children will not view a body. However, because children have vivid imaginations, what they imagine is usually more traumatic than what they actually see.

I have held a child as young as two years as I explained why we could not see his dead grandfather's legs. With only the top half of the casket open, it appeared that the body was cut off at the waist. When I opened the bottom half of the casket, the child was reassured that his grandfather's legs were still there. Other children needed to know that the reason a body felt cold was that the body had taken on room temperature, compared to our warmer body temperature. If, for some reason, a body cannot be viewed, then a careful and truthful explanation will help alleviate children's fears. Some children feel relief after viewing a body because they find that reality is less unpleasant than what they had imagined.

The sense of touch is important to children. Although Grandpa's skin is cold, they are comforted by being allowed to touch the body that they had touched so often. In instances where the body is extremely disfigured, I have found it helpful to have an arm and hand uncovered so that family members could touch and have physical contact with the dead person.

If children prefer not to view a body, their choice should be respected. They should not be forced, ridiculed, or made to feel foolish. As with any aspect of funeral rituals, children should always be allowed to remain comfortable. They should not be pushed or intimidated into situations that are stressful for them.

Funeral customs often include a time for public visitation and viewing of the body. These visitations are usually held in a funeral home, but may also be arranged in a lodge hall, church, or home. Visitation in the home, for example, tends to encourage participation of the children in the family. Wherever the visitation is held, it is important to give children the choice to spend some private time with the body. This allows them to communicate their thoughts and feelings openly and without fear of being rebuffed or rebuked. Children should also be encouraged to visit with other family members and friends, thereby allowing them to share their feelings and memories, as well as possibly learn about the memories that others have of their dead relative. Such sharing may help to strengthen their ties to the community of mourners.

During the Funeral Ceremony

There are no limits and few restrictions concerning the extent to which children, or other family members, participate in the funeral ceremony, except those enforced by family decisions, religious traditions, or clergy. I encourage children to take part in the ceremony because their participation is an excellent way for them to honor and feel connected to the person who died. I have known children to perform each of the following functions: facilitate (officiate at) the ceremony; sing and/or play a musical instrument; read Holy Scriptures or poems; eulogize and share memories of the dead person; close the casket; and carry the casket. In more traditional religious services, children bear gifts to God (signifying the return of the deceased to God), or place the pall on the casket and remove the pall from the casket. Children may also display a collage of photographs or drawings at the service.

To receive maximum social support, the bereft family should be encouraged to sit among their friends. Though funeral home "family rooms" provide privacy for family members, they also isolate those who are attempting to hide their grief from others. Such a setting does not facilitate the potential for others to provide any positive support. If family rooms are used, they should be reserved for the seating of latecomers.

During the Committal Service

Like the other dying and death procedures, burial has been turned over to the professionals. Cemetery sales persons are euphemistically called memorial counselors, and grave diggers no longer dig graves but rather open and close them. Before the burial procession arrives at the cemetery, the dirt from the grave has been secreted away, the grave is carefully covered with dyed green artificial grass matting, and there is a bright chrome lowering device on which to place the casket. During the committal service, the clergy or lodge representatives are often the only participants. After the family, friends, and clergy leave the cemetery, the artificial grass matting is removed, the casket is lowered into the grave, a lid is placed on the casket or vault, the dirt is brought back and dumped into the grave, and previously removed grass is carefully placed on top of the dirt.

It is a traditional ritual among some religious and ethnic heritages—for example, the Orthodox Jewish faith and some Native American tribes—to have family members or close friends lower the coffin into the ground, shovel dirt into the grave until it is filled, and conclude the committal service with singing and prayers. These are excellent rituals and positive ways to say good-bye and give up the person who has died. These rituals, which provide positive psychological and sociological support, can involve children and should be encouraged.

RITUALS FOR CHILDREN

Some rituals extend beyond usual funeral customs. These rituals have special meaning to children and help them solidify the social ties with their families and community. There are many such rituals, and a few of them are described below.

Drawing Pictures

Drawing pictures can provide a means for the expression of difficult feelings, especially for younger children. They should be given paper and crayons, pencils, or water colors, and encouraged to draw pictures about what they know, how they feel, and what they expect will happen. If a patient, interested older child or adult takes the time to discuss these pictures with the child, and provides positive reinforcement both for the child's drawings and feelings, this exchange may further sharing of feelings and experiences. This person should never be negative, shame the child's efforts, discredit his or her feelings, or attempt to restrict the child's expression.

Visiting the Funeral Home and/or the Church

When the funeral ceremony or any part of the funeral ritual is to be held in a funeral home or church, small children should be taken to the facility prior to the services. The purpose of this visit is to provide children with a sense of familiarity, so they will not be overwhelmed by strange and emotional activities at the time of the funeral services. During their visit, children should be told what to expect during the services, where they will be, what they will be doing, and who will be there to support them. Children should be allowed to wander about, ask questions, and receive thorough explanations in terms they can understand.

At least one funeral home has partially solved the dilemma when parents do not bring their children to visit prior to the services. Funeral directors at this mortuary provide a picture book for parents to take home to their children. This book contains pictures of the funeral home entry, chapel, family room, casket room, and so forth. Thus, children who look through the book are somewhat familiar with the funeral home prior to their arrival for the services.

Viewing the Body

Previously, I have discussed the importance of children viewing the body of someone who has died. It is also important to remember that children's questions should be encouraged, then answered honestly and directly. Such a process will allay children's fears and promote closeness and a sense of belonging. It bears repeating that children should not be denied the opportunity to view the body and participate in other segments of funeral rituals. Neither should they be forced into involvement in areas where they are uncomfortable. Children have the right to make their own choices, and those rights should be respected with regard to funeral rituals.

Visiting the Grave Site

Perhaps the most valuable interactions that I have experienced with young children have been during visits to the cemetery. I recommend that young children be taken to the cemetery, like the funeral home or church, prior to services so that the children learn what to expect during the ceremonies. They can be shown, for example, the location of their grandmother's grave, the graves of other family members, different and interesting grave markers or monuments, and a military burial section. During the committal, children at the grave site can see the depth of the grave and have their questions answered.

For both children and myself, the best experiences, however, have occurred in the days following the burials. Children are apt to feel a sense of displacement in the days and weeks following the funeral services. Because adults may be preoccupied with their own grief, children often experience confusion and are bewildered by their own feelings and the behavior of other family members. For some children, one special place to discuss these feelings and the accompanying confusion is at the cemetery.

A visit to the cemetery often provides an opportunity for children to feel close to the person who has died. At the same time, they may ask additional questions, discuss death, and voice their concerns. These visits are unique opportunities to remember the life of the one who has died, talk to that person, and relieve some of the frustrations and anxieties of recent days.

Cemetery visits also allow opportunities to establish new rituals. For instance, when several family members regularly visit the cemetery, one member may decide to be responsible for choosing and bringing flowers to the grave. In another example, each time they visit the grave, family members may take turns telling their favorite stories about the person who has died.

One of my favorite memories is of my visit to the cemetery with two little girls whose baby brother had died. We spent approximately an hour talking to their baby brother, reading and touching his tombstone, and running and jumping over a neighboring grave marker. Then we lay on our backs and watched fleecy white clouds stream across the sky, all the while talking about their family and how different family members had reacted to their baby brother's death. When we went home, we all felt better.

FURTHER RITUALS

Where there are no funeral rituals, children have no opportunity to benefit from such experiences. As a result, they may need the comfort that additional rituals can provide. Wolfelt suggests that ". . . if the funeral was somehow minimized or distorted . . ." family members may not feel that it was complete and may want to provide their own rituals [20]. Encouraging children to create their own grief rituals or memorials can help them feel better.

Children may wish, for example, to create a ritual that involves doing something special on the birth date, death date, or another special anniversary of the person who has died. They may suggest going to the zoo that they had visited with the deceased or eating at a restaurant where they had enjoyed spending time together. They may choose to watch a favorite video or prepare and eat the deceased person's favorite dessert.

Another helpful ritual for children is to memorialize the deceased by helping others. For instance, they may choose to give food to a food bank in their grandfather's memory, or make monthly visits to residents living in the nursing home where their grandmother lived and died. Following the death of a classmate, some high school students planted a tree on their school campus. The tree helps beautify the campus, and the plaque beside it commemorates the dead classmate's memory.

Children should continually be encouraged to share memories of their relationship with the person who has died and the importance of this person's life to others. These narratives help children remember and can be recalled by sharing pictures, telling stories, and remembering activities in which children and the deceased were involved. In one family, for instance, each family member was encouraged to write a memory of the person who had died and put it into a Christmas stocking. At a special gathering on Christmas Eve, the memory slips were taken from the stocking and shared with all family members.

Writing letters can also be helpful. For many years, a three-week death education unit has been included in an elective psychology class. Activities in that class involve students' own experiences. In one exercise, students write letters to express their feelings about a death in their lives. The letters are written to anyone they wish, including the person who has died. When completed, the letters are sealed with the assurance that no one will ever see their contents. The next day, students place their letters into a fire, and the letters are consumed by the flames.

Evidence that this activity is a positive experience was relayed by participants who described the letter writing and burning as "an excellent idea" or "a wonderful idea." Others stated, "I felt a sense of relief when I saw the envelope being engulfed in flames and taken away forever" and "[W]hen I set my letter on the flames and it began to burn, I felt relief. At first, I was unsure if I was ready to let it go, but when I did, it felt good." Finally, one student reported that burning the letter ". . . made me feel like I was cleaning a refrigerator with lots of old leftovers" [21, pp. 274-275].

A SUMMARY OF SUGGESTIONS FOR PERSONALIZING
FUNERAL CEREMONIES FOR CHILDREN

> If we can begin to prepare the adolescent in childhood for funeral practices and other social rituals surrounding death . . . we will do much to lift the taboo attached to dying people, bereaved survivors, cemeteries, dead bodies, and funeral procedures [22, p. 24].

It should be apparent that rituals are important to all family members, but perhaps more necessary for children. It is the children who need the social support and security that rituals provide. Rituals give children confidence that they are connected with the past, belong to the present, and can look forward to the future. The following suggestions will help to personalize funeral ceremonies for children:

1. We must involve families more, funeral directors and clergy less. Funeral directors and clergy are important facilitators, but funeral rituals are not as important for them as for the families of those who have died. These families should be the designers of, and participants in, the funeral. Siblings, children, and grandchildren should be encouraged to participate in the funeral ceremony.
2. Families, including children, should be surrounded by the loving support of their friends and the community. They should not be hidden in a separate room during funeral rituals.
3. Just as children and other family members are encouraged to participate in the funeral, so should they be encouraged to participate in the burial ceremony. They can, for example, read a poem or sing a song, help lower the casket, or throw dirt into the grave.
4. Children should be urged to commemorate the dead person during special holiday and anniversary occasions. For younger children, pictures of the deceased are helpful in recalling memories of that person. One company in Spokane, Washington, produces an excellent six minute video that combines fifteen pictures of the deceased with nature scenes and background music. This "Tribute" program is available through many funeral homes.
5. Personal rituals at home that involve children should be encouraged. For instance, children could light a candle on the

anniversary of their grandfather's death or eat his favorite pie on the occasion of his birthday.

Children participating in rituals are likely to gain considerable psychological and emotional comfort from such involvement. They will experience a sense of belonging and feel they have contributed to their family and the community. Most importantly, children must be included in death rituals because these rituals demonstrate the continuity of society while illustrating the fact that life moves forward, even though an important person in their lives has died.

REFERENCES

1. U.S. Bureau of the Census, *Statistical Abstract of the United States: 1993* (113th Edition), Washington, D.C., 1993.
2. L. L. Bumpass, Children and Marital Disruption: A Replication and Update, *Demography, 14*, pp. 71-82, 1984.
3. R. Bendiksen and R. Fulton, Death and the Child: An Antrospective Test of the Childhood Bereavement and Later Behavior Disorder Hypothesis, in *Death and Identity* (Rev. Edition), R. Fulton and R. Bendiksen (eds.), The Charles Press, Bowie, Maryland, pp. 274-287, 1976.
4. P. R. Amato and A. Booth, Consequences of Parental Divorce and Marital Unhappiness for Adult Well-being, *Social Forces, 69*:3, pp. 895-914, 1991.
5. J. Kunz, The Effects of Divorce on Children, *Family Research: A Sixty-year Review, 1930-1990*, Vol. 2, S. Bahr (ed.), Lexington Books, New York, pp. 325-376, 1991.
6. J. S. Wallerstein and S. Blakeslee, *Second Chances: Men, Women, and Children A Decade After Divorce*, Ticknor and Fields, New York, 1989.
7. A. Z. Schwartzberg, The Impact of Divorce on Adolescents, *Hospital and Community Psychiatry, 43*:6, pp. 634-637, 1992.
8. O. D. Weeks, *AIDS in the 1990s: The Risk for University Students*, unpublished doctoral dissertation, Minneapolis, Minnesota, 1994.
9. C. M. Sanders, *Grief, the Mourning After*, John Wiley and Sons, New York, 1989.
10. T. A. Rando, *Grief, Dying, and Death, Clinical Interventions for Caregivers*, Research Press Company, Champaign, Illinois, 1984.
11. L. A. DeSpelder and A. L. Strickland, *The Last Dance* (2nd Edition), Mayfield Publishing Company, Palo Alto, California, 1987.
12. R. W. Habenstein and W. M. Lamers, *The History of American Funeral Directing* (Rev. Edition), Bulfin Printers, Inc., Milwaukee, Wisconsin, 1962.
13. Genesis 23:4, *New International Version of The Holy Bible*, Zondervan Bible Publishers, Grand Rapids, Michigan, 1978.
14. Ecclesiastes 6:3, *New International Version of The Holy Bible*, Zondervan Bible Publishers, Grand Rapids, Michigan, 1978.

15. B. B. Hess, E. W. Markson, and P. J. Stein, *Sociology* (4th Edition), 1993 Update, Macmillan Publishing Company, New York, 1993.

16. D. T. Manning, N. Barenberg, L. Gallese, and J. Rice, College Students' Knowledge and Health Beliefs about AIDS: Implication for Education and Prevention, *Journal of American College Health, 37*, pp. 254-259, 1989.

17. J. W. Eddy and W. F. Alles, *Death Education*, The C. V. Mosby Company, St. Louis, Missouri, 1983.

18. J. W. Worden, *Grief Counseling and Grief Therapy*, Springer Publishing Company, New York, 1982.

19. L. Carlson, *Caring for Your Own Dead*, Upper Access Publishers, Hinesburg, Vermont, 1987.

20. A. D. Wolfelt, *Understand Grief: Helping Yourself Heal*, Accelerated Development Publishers Inc., Muncie, Indiana, 1992.

21. O. D. Weeks and C. L. Johnson, A Second Decade of High School Death Education, *Death Studies, 16*:2, pp. 269-279, 1992.

22. A. K. Gordon, The Tattered Cloak of Immortality, in *Adolescence and Death*, C. Corr and J. McNeil (eds.), Springer Publishing Company, New York, pp. 16-31, 1986.

CHAPTER 11

Do Children Belong at Funerals?

Bunty Anderson

The question, "Do children belong at funerals?" is rarely debated in the mental health community. As professional helpers, our experience and intuition tell us that, of course, children belong at funerals—what is the issue? The clinical literature that examines this topic offers us a broad consensus that supports children being included in the rituals of death. For example, Rando [1] in *Grieving: How To Go On When Someone You Love Dies* and Raphael's book [2] *Anatomy Of Bereavement* provide numerous examples of the value of including children in funerals. Where then, does this question come from?

As a medical social worker, I hear this question from families struggling to cope with life-threatening illnesses and death. What may be a straightforward issue for the professional helper becomes a difficult decision for families facing the question of whether to include their children in the rituals of death. Clinical rhetoric and research lose their meaning as the family imagines their *own* children at their *own* loved one's funeral. The challenge for the clinician is to be informed and guided by the theoretical literature, while honoring and respecting the poignancy of the family's experience.

Throughout this chapter, I will integrate clinical literature with case examples; examine the roles played by funerals and consider the importance of these roles or functions for children; and discuss children as disadvantaged grievers in order to sensitize ourselves to the special issues which children bring to the grieving process. A review will follow of common concerns that adult family members often voice when debating children's attendance at funerals. Finally, there will be an in-depth discussion of interventions. This will focus on how to prepare children so that the funeral is an emotionally manageable experience.

THE ROLES AND FUNCTIONS OF FUNERALS FOR CHILDREN

The conviction that children belong at funerals deserves further examination. Why do they belong?

A funeral is an important occasion in a family's life. People come together to mark the momentous change that occurs as the family system is confronted with death. Just as we do not automatically exclude children from other family milestones such as weddings, graduations, bar mitzvahs, or baptisms, they should not be excluded from funerals.

Funerals are an important source of ritual. As the twentieth century draws to a close, we see a style of life that has become increasingly hectic and fragmented. Rituals are needed more now than ever, especially by children. Rites, rituals and ceremonies provide us with a framework for our experience and give us the opportunity to work through our feelings.

Funerals also serve several important functions. They are a concrete statement that the death has actually happened. The ceremony of leavetaking confirms and reinforces the reality that we so naturally wish to deny.

Even though there may be no emotional acceptance of the death at the time of the funeral, over time memories of the experience will help to confirm that the death actually occurred. For example:

> Ryan, a twelve-year-old boy, was a passenger in a car being driven by his mother. Their car was broadsided by a pick-up truck, and his mother was killed instantly. Ryan was seriously injured, and remained in hospital for two months after the accident. During a discussion of funeral experiences in a teen bereavement group, Ryan told us that he knew his mother was dead. However, he really did not believe it because he never saw her dead, never attended the funeral, and never saw her buried.

Because funerals elicit many grief reactions, it is important for children to have the opportunity to witness the expression of strong emotions. The responses of other people provide children with role models for the grieving behavior that is characteristic of their social or ethnic culture. For example, if adults react to events with a stiff upper lip, children may restrict the expression of their own emotions and experience confusion about whether their own responses are normal. The funeral experience offers children the opportunity to observe that emotions are a normal, expected response to death, and that such expression is acceptable.

Funerals serve the additional function of facilitating input from the community about the person's life beyond the family. This helps mourners round out their picture of the deceased and is especially important for children who have not had the time or opportunity to know every facet of a loved parent or relative before death. Being present at the storytelling and memorializing that takes place at a funeral helps to integrate and broaden the picture of the deceased. This is an important aspect of the grieving process and is evident in the following example:

> David was fourteen years old when he witnessed his father's death in a snowmobile accident. His father had been an extremely successful business man who had spent much of David's childhood away from home, building his business. In bereavement, David spent considerable time grieving the fact that he had not had time to get to know his Dad. At the funeral, David was amazed by the numbers of people who attended, and the lives that had been touched by his father.

Finally, the funeral provides the community with the opportunity to offer condolences, share the loss, and provide social and emotional support to the family. Through the manifestation of shared loss, it is affirmed to the family that they are not alone in their grief. Children frequently talk about the difficulty they experienced when they returned to school after a death. "Who knows?", "Who doesn't know?", and "Will I be treated differently?" are common concerns. The path back into the social group is eased by the support offered by others.

> Daniel was twelve and Heather was ten years old when their mother was killed in a car accident. Although they attended the same school, their classroom teachers had differing views on how to respond to this tragedy. Daniel's teacher closed her classroom on the afternoon of the funeral and the whole class attended the service. Heather's teacher barely acknowledged the event and went about business as usual: None of Heather's peers shared the funeral experience. This disparity created a tremendous amount of unnecessary pain for Heather. After the funeral, Heather told me, "I hated all the attention that Daniel got from his friends and teacher. It felt like nobody cared about me."

CHILDREN AS DISADVANTAGED GRIEVERS

Having reviewed some of the many reasons why children belong at funerals, it is also important to be aware of the ways in which children are disadvantaged as grievers [1, p. 200; 3, p. 201]. This awareness will help health professionals prepare families to understand how children's grief differs from their own. Children are aided in their ability to mourn when the adults around them are sensitive to their unique issues.

Cognitive development plays an important role in how children respond to death. Young children are disadvantaged because of their immature thinking ability. They are great observers but poor interpreters, often making inaccurate generalizations [1, p. 200]. For example:

> Jordan's mother was dying of cancer. Throughout the course of her illness, the cancer was never named directly, but rather referred to as the "disease." After her death, six-year-old Jordan wept uncontrollably. He told his father that he never wanted to hear of anyone getting a disease in his family again—only a cold or the flu would be okay.

Children are also disadvantaged in their grief work because they have not yet developed the ability to verbally express their emotions and describe their experience. Telling one's story, reminiscing, and expressing feelings are all important tasks when integrating and working through grief. The natural limitations of children's development may slow their grieving process [1, p. 200].

Children are also disadvantaged grievers because they have access to fewer resources and available options as compared to adults. Accustomed to depending on family members for emotional support and nurturing, children are apt to find family members emotionally absent or unavailable because they are immersed in their own grief [1, p. 201]. Emotional support from peers is usually inadequate or unavailable. Unlike adults, children are not likely to take a compassionate leave from school, take a "mental health" day, or have their daily tasks temporarily assumed by others. In short, the coping options and resources available to children are dramatically limited [1, p. 201].

In addition to the above, children are at a disadvantage because they lack exposure to experiences that teach them that pain gradually subsides and life goes on [1, p. 201]. The cataclysmic event of death is life-shattering for children. Death experienced in childhood may create disruption in the child's sense of security and view of the world as a good, safe place. My clinical experience with adults who were bereaved as children suggest that they often live in fear, "waiting for the other shoe to fall." It is as though they can never feel safe and secure again. Unlike adults, children can seldom understand death by comparing it to the deaths experienced by their peers. Most children in my bereavement groups have told me, "I'm the only kid in my class with a dead Mom."

Another way in which children are disadvantaged relates to their inability to grieve intensely for long periods of time [1, p. 201]. I believe that this creates at least two problems. First, mourning extends for a very long time as children's understanding of death changes and there is a need to ask questions and clarify facts. Second, children are apt to suffer guilt and confusion when they notice that they are not behaving as adults expect them to behave [1, p. 206]. For example:

> Sandra was almost eight years old when her Dad died after a two year battle with cancer. A first-born child, she was serious and responsible beyond her years and carried an air of sadness about her. She told me that sometimes she would be at her friend's house so busy playing and laughing that she would forget her Dad had died. Her worried eyes filled with tears while she watched me, waiting for my response.

Finally, children are particularly vulnerable to the secondary losses resulting from a death [1, p. 203]. Their mourning is twofold, especially when death occurs in the immediate family. They mourn the person who has died and they mourn the emotional absence of their usual caregivers. Children are often left with family members who are so emotionally drained by the death that they are unavailable in significant ways, at least for a period of time. Many children in my bereavement groups have commented that they refrain from sharing their own feelings because, "It makes my Mom cry when I talk about it." One topic covered in our bereavement group is, "What changes have happened in your family since the death?" The children are able to eloquently articulate the secondary losses following a death:

> *Natalie (eight years old)*:
> "Since my sister died, my Mom doesn't want us to celebrate Christmas."
> *Jim (eleven years old)*:
> "We don't have family gatherings at our house any more—we go to our Auntie's instead."
> *David (ten years old)*:
> "My Mom can't go out in the evening since my Dad died because there's no one to stay with us."

Suzanne (fourteen years old):
"My Mom died in September and when my birthday came around
in November, there was no cake and no present. My Dad forgot."

ADULT FAMILY MEMBERS: SOME COMMON CONCERNS

Understanding the ways in which children are disadvantaged
grievers enhances our sensitivity to their needs and issues. Parents
bring special concerns to the experience of death, especially when their
own children are involved. By carefully listening to their protests and
worries over their children's attendance at a funeral, the practitioner
can often work successfully with their resistance so that children are
given the opportunity to be included in the rituals of death.

A declaration commonly heard is, "a funeral is no place for a child."
Respectful listening is always the best beginning. The clinician must
assume a compassionate stance, encouraging adults to identify their
fears and concerns. The opportunity to vent emotion and explain their
thinking on the matter often results in talking themselves out of their
original position. Openness and receptivity on the practitioner's part
help to minimize any defensive stance taken by parents.

When discussing their doubts about a child's funeral attendance,
adults often support their position by stating, "I was never allowed at
funerals when I was a child." One person was gently disarmed by the
question, "What was it like for you to be left out of funerals when you
were small?" The response described feeling angry, resentful, left out,
and de-valued. Not attending the funeral of her beloved aunt was
experienced as "on-going unfinished business." Many adults describe
feeling tremendous fear when they must attend a funeral for the first
time later in their lives.

Other common concerns expressed by adults include children are
"too young for all this sadness" or "too young to understand." These
issues can also be addressed compassionately. The practitioner can
remind parents that children are not sheltered from sadness when they
do not attend a funeral. The opportunity to experience sadness at a
funeral is better than to be left to cope with the anxiety of the unknown.
As Grollman points out, that which is known is always more manageable than the fantasized unknown [4, p. 25]. Although children may be
"too young to understand" in the same way that adults do, they are,
nevertheless, masters at sensing and reacting to nuance and emotional
tone. We do best when we seize the opportunity, provide adequate
explanation, and include them in the rituals of death.

Another stumbling block for many adults is that they do not want their children to see them "break down at the funeral." Many adults carry injunctions about "being strong" or "keeping a stiff upper lip." These adults can be helped to understand that "breaking down" is an appropriate grief response. It teaches children that emotional expression is permitted.

Some families are concerned that attendance at the funeral will give their child nightmares. However, there is no guarantee that a child's dreams will be idyllic if he does not attend the funeral. If children do experience nightmares, discussing them may provide another opportunity to share feelings and grieve together.

Listening carefully, exploring the meaning of an adult client's childhood experience, and reframing, are all useful tools for the clinician. However, it is important to remember the heart of the matter: Adults want to protect children from this overwhelming experience. Protecting them is a basic and profound need which must be honored in the therapeutic setting. Discovering our inability to protect children from pain elicits a sense of helplessness and despair. We must remind adults that, although we cannot keep children from suffering, we can keep them from suffering for the wrong reasons.

Finally, we must be aware that the clinician who listens to adult concerns calmly and respectfully is an implicit model for parents who, in turn, can offer the same compassionate listening to their children.

PREPARING CHILDREN FOR FUNERALS

So far, we have articulated the roles and functions of funerals and why it is important for children to attend. We have sought to sensitize ourselves to the special issues children bring to the grieving experience, and we have explored ways to intervene with adults who resist children's attendance at funerals. How can we help families prepare children to attend funerals?

In order to make children's funeral experiences emotionally manageable, it is important to provide them with explanations that they can easily understand. This is easier said than done! What makes explanations so difficult? What do children need to know?

It may be more difficult to provide clear explanations because children possess a different level of cognitive understanding. Children tend to repeat their questions over time, trying to make sense of what has happened. They are partly seeking reassurance that the answers have not changed, and they are attempting to integrate a greater understanding of what has transpired, in keeping with the changes in their ability to think rationally. For example:

> Karl was six years old and his siblings were aged three, six, and nine when he was diagnosed with a brain tumour and died within six months. The family dealt with the death in a very open manner, frequently mentioning Karl's name. Four years after the death, the youngest child (now 7 years old) wanted to know if his dead brother was still able to play hockey in heaven. He also wondered if he had his birthday in heaven and would he still be six or was he ten now?

Explanations are further complicated by the fact that concepts of time and futurity often elude children. The expression "a long time" has a different meaning to children of different ages. The father of a four-year-old girl was surprised at how well his daughter was taking the news of her mother's death from ovarian cancer. She cried very little and said even less. Four days after the death she announced to her Dad, "I want you to go to the hospital and get Mommy. She's been dead long enough."

Another poignant example of difficulty with the concept of time was illustrated by a five-year-old boy, whose mother had been hospitalized for just over a month. He described in a voice full of longing, "My Mom was in the hospital for a thousand weeks."

In the quest to offer solid explanations to children, adults can be guided by an awareness of children's needs. In the face of death, these needs are straightforward; they need truthful, honest information about what is happening. Without such information, they will be left insecure and wondering what else they have not been told. Children need age-appropriate information about death. Describing death as a biological process is best, and comparisons can be made by alluding to a broken toy, or a car engine with a stone in it. After death, the body can be likened to a school building without the students, a shell without the peanut, or a glove without a hand. Children need to be told information immediately so they do not hear it indirectly from someone else [1, p. 212]. For example:

> Melanie was a fifteen-year-old from a small, rural town. When Melanie's Mom was diagnosed with breast cancer, she could not bring herself to tell her children and instead discussed the diagnosis with friends. The adult friends, not realizing that the children did not know, talked with their own children about the tragedy. Melanie learned about her Mom's cancer from her classmates at school. Eighteen months later, in a teen bereavement group, Melanie was still upset and angry about how she had learned the truth.

Children need to know they are loved and will continue to be cared for—despite their parents' upset. Maintaining a routine is very important and reassuring for children. They need someone to anticipate and understand their feelings, and they need to know that their difficult feelings will not last forever. Having an adult anticipate feelings provides children with an emotional road map, a sense of what to expect, and what is normal. It can be particularly helpful for adults to acknowledge feelings which seem contradictory and may be interpreted as "bad." For example, children may be upset by feeling relieved when a beloved parent dies after a protracted illness filled with suffering.

Once adults have prepared them for what they may see and feel, children need the opportunity to view the body. However, they should not be forced to do so against their will. They will often follow the lead of a parent, grandparent, or older sibling who provides them with comfort and reassurance.

> Jennifer was fourteen years old when her grandfather died from cancer. At the hospital, she was given the option to view her grandfather's body. "My Mom wanted me to look but I felt I couldn't stand it. I'm really sorry now 'cause I know I'll never have that chance again."

> Michael was ten when his father died unexpectedly of a heart attack. He went with his family to the emergency room at the hospital, where he had a chance to view the body. "At the hospital, my Dad looked and felt the same. I hugged him but he didn't hug back—then I knew he was really dead."

Children need to know they are not to blame and are not responsible for the death. They need to be reassured that nothing they did, said, or wished for could have caused the person to die. For example:

> Alan was fourteen years old when his Dad died suddenly from a heart attack. In a teen bereavement group session, he said, "I know that heart attacks are caused by stress. Sometimes I'd lie to my Dad about things and he would get pretty mad at me." Alan needed lots of reassurance that his lying had not caused his father's heart attack.

Finally, children need permission from adults to mourn [1, p. 216]. If this is not received, children will work hard at protecting the adults in their lives from the pain of witnessing their grief.

In addition to examining what children need from adults, it is important to consider what they do not need. The following is a brief checklist of what to avoid:

1. Do not be evasive. Children do best when they receive honest, straightforward information.
2. Avoid philosophical abstractions. These may only confuse children. Simple is best.
3. Avoid stories or fairy tales about death. For example, do not refer to Grandma as now having shiny angel wings. Grollman points out that this only serves to confuse children who may already be having difficulty distinguishing between what is real and what is pretend [4].
4. Avoid any untruth that will have to be unlearned later. It is important to be careful not to use euphemistic explanations that confuse or frighten children. For example, telling children that, "Mother has gone on a long journey" may well result in children being terrified of trips. Explaining "God took Dad to heaven because he was so good" may motivate children to be bad so that they can avoid the same fate. And predictably, referring to death as eternal sleep can pave the way for bedtime problems.
5. Avoid any explanations that you do not believe. It is probably best to avoid theological explanations and focus instead on the emotional meaning for the mourner. Grollman calls this a focus on spiritual development rather than theological doctrine [4].

A powerful example of the literal-minded child's confusion with theological explanation is found in this excerpt from a poem by Manitoba writer Di Brandt:

> . . . look when grampa died last week everybody said he's better off where he is because he's in heaven now he's with God we should be happy he's gone home but yesterday when they put him in the ground the minister said he's going to be there till the last trumpet raises the quick and the dead for the final judgement now look mom i can't figure which is true it's got to be either up or down i mean what's he gonna do swoop back into his body at the last moment so he can rise with the trumpet call or what i got to know mom what do you think . . . [6, p. 5].

Funeral attendance can be emotionally manageable when thoughtfully handled by caring adults. The principle of inclusion recommends that the child be offered the choice to attend. In my experience, children seldom need encouragement to attend a funeral; they are usually anxious to be included.

It is important to prepare children for what they will see at the funeral. Be sure to mention that others may be crying and upset and that this is a natural way to respond when someone is grieving. Once you have finished your explanation, listen carefully to all questions and answer them truthfully and simply.

Some families assign a back-up adult who will be ready to take care of the children in case they become overwhelmed and wish to leave. This back-up adult acts as a safety valve. The identity and function of this person should be explained to the child prior to the funeral. It should be someone who is well known to the child, and not a member of the immediate family. It is important that family members have the opportunity to complete the funeral and attend to their own grief.

If children choose not to attend the funeral, their wishes should be respected. It is also advisable to include children in other mourning rituals. For example, they may wish to visit the cemetery, contribute to a memorial fund, or be assigned to answer the door when people come visiting. In short, find an important role for the child to play.

If a child is unable to attend the funeral because of illness, hospitalization, or other circumstances, it is helpful to have some tangible evidence of the funeral. Suggestions include taking photographs, taping the funeral, or perhaps taking a lock of hair from the deceased.

CONCLUSION

A Case Study

The question in this chapter's title was most vividly brought to my attention through my work with one particular family. This family's story contains an illustration of all the issues discussed in this chapter.

Mr. G., fifty-eight years of age, had been living for eighteen months with a diagnosis of pancreatic cancer. At the time of our first meeting, the cancer had spread extensively and he was in the terminal stages of this disease. Mr. and Mrs. G. had enjoyed a long marriage of thirty-five years and had two adult daughters. Both daughters were in their early thirties, married, and each had three young children. As the time for Mr. G.'s death drew near, the six grandchildren, ages ranging from three to ten years old, became the focus of a heated disagreement among the family members. The children's grandmother, strongly believed that the children should be kept away from the death bed at the hospital and should definitely not attend the funeral. However, the children were keen to see their grandfather at the hospital and their mothers supported their request. Their grandfather was too ill to participate in the discussion.

After the daughters approached me with this problem, I invited Mrs. G. to share her concerns about her grandchildren. She worried that the children would be afraid and would have nightmares. She was sure that they were too young for all this sadness and that they did not really understand what was happening. They certainly should not be attending the funeral. When she was a child she had never been allowed to attend funerals. Finally, she raised her main concern. She was afraid of the children's reactions if she was to "break down" in front of them. Slowly, over several days, these concerns were labeled and patiently addressed with her.

As their father's condition deteriorated, one of the daughters enlisted the help of the family's rabbi. Mrs. G. heard the rabbi echo similar beliefs and approaches to those that had been addressed by myself and her daughters. She relented and allowed the children one last visit with their beloved grandfather.

After the hospital visit, the mothers discussed the grandfather's impending death with their children. The six children had only a few questions, then left the room to play on the family's computer. Within an hour, they returned with the following written tribute which clearly demonstrated their understanding, their need to be included, and their need to commemorate their grandfather. Four days later, the children were present at his funeral where their tribute was read to the mourners:

DEDICATED TO OUR ZAIDA SYL, WITH LOVE

I love my Zaida because . . .

Pamela (age 5 1/2): He took me for ice cream
He is handsome
He is very nice to me
He did things for me
He played with me
He tied my shoes when I didn't know how
He taught me how to ride my bike
He helped me when I needed it

Justin (age 6): He taught me how to play chess
He gave me a fishing rod
He played with me

He got me things
He did me favors
He took me places
He took me fishing
He helped me fly my kite
He helped me with my math
He means a lot to me

Stephanie (age 5): He is important to me

Shoshana (age 8): He is always nice to me
He got me things
He means a lot to me
He taught me how to play chess and
  checkers
He took me on bike rides
He is very special to me

Melissa (age 10): He is very special to me
He means a lot to me
He took me on bike rides
He took me for ice cream
He took me for walks
He played with me
He is very nice to me
He taught me how to play checkers and
  chess

Hadarah (age 3): He always listens to my stories

What I did for my Zaida . . .

Pamela: I did him favors

Justin: I kept him company
I helped him
I played with him
I made things for him

Stephanie: I helped him
I did things for him

Shoshana: I found the t.v. remote for him
I did him a favor
I filled his water bottle for him without him
knowing

Melissa: I taught him how to play nintendo
I made him things
I did things for him—walk the dog
I kept him company
I loved him

Hadarah: I read him stories
I kept him company

I am sad because . . .

Pamela: My Zaida is going to die soon
He has cancer

Justin: My Zaida has cancer
He is dying

Stephanie: My Zaida has cancer
My Zaida is going to die

Shoshana: My Zaida can't come home
My Zaida has cancer
My Zaida is going to die soon
I will miss him

Melissa: He is going to die
He has cancer
There is no cure for cancer
I'm going to really miss him
I will never see him again after he dies
I won't be able to do things with him

Hadarah: I'm going to miss him very much
I won't be able to read him stories any
more.

REFERENCES

1. T. A. Rando, *Grieving: How To Go On Living When Someone You Love Dies*, Lexington Books, D.C. Heath and Company, Lexington, Massachusetts, 1988.
2. B. Raphael, *The Anatomy Of Bereavement*, Basic Books, Inc., New York, 1983.
3. R. R. Ellis, Young Children: Disenfranchised Grievers, in *Disenfranchised Grief*, Kenneth Doka (ed.), Lexington Books, D.C. Heath and Co., Lexington, Massachusetts, 1989.
4. E. Grollman, *Explaining Death To Children*, Beacon Press, Boston, 1967.
5. E. Grollman, Children And Death, in *Concerning Death: A Practical Guide For The Living*, E. Grollman (ed.), Beacon Press, Boston, 1974.
6. Di Brandt, *Questions I Asked My Mother*, Turnstone Press, Winnipeg, 1987. (used with permission)

About the Editors

David W. Adams, M.S.W., C.S.W. is a Professor, Department of Psychiatry, Faculty of Health Sciences, McMaster University and Executive Director, Greater Hamilton Employee Assistance Consortium. Over the past 25 years in his affiliation with Chedoke-McMaster Hospitals and McMaster University, he has concentrated much of clinical social work practice and teaching on life-threatening illness, dying, death and bereavement in childhood and the impact on children and families. He is the author of *Childhood Malignancy: The Psychosocial Care of the Child and His Family* and *Parents of Children with Cancer Speak Out: Needs, Problems, and Sources of Help*. David is co-author with Ellie Deveau of *Coping with Childhood Cancer: Where Do We Go From Here?* He is a charter member of the board and Chair, Professional Advisors of the Candlelighters Childhood Cancer Foundation Canada, Chair of the International Work Group on Death, Dying and Bereavement and past Chair, Psychosocial Services Committee of the Pediatric Oncology Group of Ontario. David is a certified death educator and grief counsellor. He has contributed numerous chapters and articles and is internationally known as a speaker, program consultant, and workshop facilitator.

Eleanor (Ellie) J. Deveau, R.N., B.Sc.N. is coordinator of program evaluation in the Educational Center for Aging and Health, Faculty of Health Sciences, McMaster University, Hamilton, Ontario, Canada. She is bereavement consultant and advisor to Friends in Grief, Inc., Hamilton, Ontario and a founding member of their board of directors. Ellie is a certified death educator through the Association of Death Education and Counseling (USA) and a member of the International Work Group on Death, Dying and Bereavement. Many years of experience as a nurse practitioner in the pediatric hematology/oncology program at McMaster University Medical Center led to her co-authorship of the award-winning book, *Coping with Childhood Cancer: Where Do We Go From Here?* Ellie is a speaker and workshop facilitator and has contributed chapters and articles which focus on issues relating to children and adolescents' understanding of death, the impact of life-threatening illness and palliative care on children, siblings and parents, the pattern of grief in children and adolescents, and child and adult bereavement.

Contributors

BUNTY ANDERSON, B.S.W., Oncology Social Worker, Manitoba Cancer Treatment and Research Foundation, Winnipeg, Manitoba, Canada.

CHARLES A. CORR, Ph.D., Professor, School of Humanities, Southern Illinois University at Edwardsville, Edwardsville, Illinois, United States.

GERRY R. COX, Ph.D., Professor of Sociology, South Dakota School of Mines and Technology, Rapid City, South Dakota, United States.

LYNNE ANN DeSPELDER, M.A., Instructor, Cabrillo College, Aptos, California; Educator, Author, and Counselor, Capitola, California, United States.

ELEANOR J. DEVEAU, R.N., B.Sc.N., Coordinator, Program Evaluation, Educational Centre for Aging and Health, Faculty of Health Sciences, McMaster University; Bereavement Consultant, Friends in Grief, Inc., Hamilton, Ontario, Canada.

ROBERT FULTON, Ph.D., Professor of Sociology, Director, Center for Death Education and Research, Department of Sociology, University of Minnesota, Minneapolis, Minnesota, United States.

RONALD J. FUNDIS, Ph.M., Vice President and Assistant to the President; Sociologist, Policy Analyst, and College Senior Administrator, Jefferson College, Hillsboro, Missouri, United States.

EARL A. GROLLMAN, D.D., Clergy, Author, and Lecturer, Belmont, Massachusetts, United States.

IDA M. MARTINSON, R.N., Ph.D., F.A.A.N., Professor, Department of Family Health Care Nursing, School of Nursing, University of California at San Francisco, San Francisco, California, United States.

PATRICK J. McGINNIS, B.A., Assistant Researcher, Docking Institute of Public Affairs; Instructor of Sociology, Fort Hays State University, Hays, Kansas, United States.

JUDITH M. STILLION, Ph.D., M.A., B.S., Vice Chancellor for Academic Affairs; Professor of Psychology, Western Carolina University, Cullowhee, North Carolina, United States.

ALBERT LEE STRICKLAND, Author and Editor, Capitola, Calfornia, United States.

BERNARD J. VANDEN BERK, M.Ed., Teacher, Valley View Elementary School, Ashwanbenon School District, Ashwanbenon, Wisconsin, United States.

HANNELORE WASS, Ph.D., Professor Emeritus, Educational Psychology; Associate, Center for Gerontological Studies, University of Florida, Gainesville, Florida, United States.

O. DUANE WEEKS, Ph.D., President and Funeral Director, Weeks' Funeral Homes, Inc., Buckley, Washington, United States.

Index

A

Abandonment, feeling of, 58, 153
Abortion, 90, 128
Abstraction, use of, 58, 74, 87, 172
Acute grief responses, 147
Adolescence/Adolescent, 49, 68,
    71-74, 95
  abstract thought and reasoning,
      50, 58, 59, 64, 72, 74, 85-87
  aggressive/violent behavior, 35,
      36, 39, 104, 110
  anxieties concerning death, 23,
      34, 35, 74, 84, 87,
  causes/incidence of death in, 19,
      30, 33, 39
  cognitive development, 22, 58-59,
      64, 71-74, 75, 145
  death, 19, 35, 73
  death of a friend, 3, 55, 73, 74,
      89
  death of a relative, 2, 34, 55, 74,
      153, 171
  dying, 2, 127
  emotional development, 22, 50,
      59, 71-74, 145, 147
  existential concerns, 74
  feelings, 22, 34, 35, 73, 74, 87
  gender differences, 34, 37, 103
  independence, 34, 71-72, 145-146,
      147, 151
  invulnerability, 23, 129
  peer relationships, 23, 71-72, 89,
      99, 103, 150

[Adolescence/Adolescent]
  perceptions of death, 23, 72,
      84-85, 87, 89-90, 97, 105
  phases/stages, 71-72, 74, 75
  rebellion, 71, 145
  risk-taking behavior, 23, 46, 72,
      102, 105, 124-125, 126, 127,
      129
  sexuality, 71, 72, 124-126, 128,
      129
  suicide, 2, 19, 35-37, 39, 73, 89,
      102,
  understanding of death, 59, 64,
      75, 90, 159
Adult (*see also* Parent)
  attitudes toward death, 13, 17,
      18, 19, 110, 149, 163, 168
  feelings during bereavement, 157,
      163, 166-167, 168, 170-171
  protective role, 9, 18, 163, 168,
      169
  role in death education, 3, 10, 11,
      17-18, 25, 26, 46-49, 51, 55,
      57, 170, 171
  understanding of death, 10, 11,
      17, 18, 21, 26, 48, 63, 169, 171
Advertising, impact of, 98, 100, 106
Advocacy groups, 98, 100, 101, 102,
      103, 105, 106, 128
Afterlife, 69, 72, 74, 84, 86, 87, 148
Aggression/Aggressive behavior,
      (*see also* Violence)
    adolescent, 35, 36, 39, 104, 110
    biological basis for, 35-36, 40

183

[Aggression/Aggressive behavior]
  definition, 35-36
  environmental/social basis for,
    33, 40, 105
  gender differences in, 3-4, 5, 30,
    33, 35-37, 39, 103, 109, 110,
    113
  in play, games, and toys, 4, 24,
    36, 100, 113
  research on, 34-35, 97, 102, 109,
    110, 115
  school intervention program, 40
AIDS (HIV), 1, 2, 5, 123-130, 145
  death, 127, 129, 157
  epidemic, 123, 127, 129
  research on, 46, 124, 128
  risks, 124, 127
  role of media, 123, 128-129
  student's understanding of, 46,
    124, 126
Alcohol abuse (see also Drug and
    alcohol abuse)
  among youth, 102, 105, 128
Alopecia, in childhood cancer, 140
Ancestors, 145
Anger, 112, 168, 170
Animal death, (see Pet)
Anxiety, 49, 66, 68, 69, 73, 75, 138,
    168, 173
  about death, 3, 9, 12, 23, 29, 34,
    35, 47, 50, 55, 57, 74, 75, 84,
    87, 95, 168
Artwork, 4, 155, 196
  age-related, 65-71, 72, 75, 77-88,
    112
  gender differences, 70, 75, 112,
    113
  characteristics of, 65, 67, 68,
    69-70, 71, 75, 77-87,
  colors used in, 67, 75, 80, 86,
    87
  medium for expressing feelings,
    65, 112, 113, 115
  portrayal of death in, 21, 65, 72,
    75, 76, 77-87, 88, 89
  portrayal of violence/war in, 110,
    112, 113, 115, 118-121

[Artwork]
  research on, 65-70, 74, 77-86,
    88-90
  symbols/symbolism used in, 68,
    70, 75, 82, 86
Avoidance of death, 3, 11, 21, 50,
    51, 55, 56, 67, 142, 150, 151,
    172, (see also Taboo)

B

Banishment of death, 56 (see also
    Avoidance of death; Taboo)
Bedtime fears, 34, 172
Bereaved child, 2, 3, 4, 5, 9, 11, 12,
    16, 18, 24, 25, 26, 34, 49, 127
  gender differences, 34-35
  participation in funeral and
    rituals of burial, 145-160,
    163-176
Bereavement support group, 3, 26,
    164, 167, 170, 171
Bodily functions, cessation of, 50,
    58, 59, 60, 61, 67, 69, 73
Body
  after death, 20, 58, 70, 81, 83, 87,
    148, 149, 150, 152, 153
  mutilation, 50, 68, 75, 96, 99
  preparation after death, 20, 148,
    153
  viewing after death, 153, 154,
    156, 171
Bone marrow transplantation, 139
Buddhism, 133, 134, 141
Burial, 70, 86, 147, 150, 155, 156
  child's participation in, 159
  fear of, 70
  practices, 69, 88, 149
  rituals/rites, 4, 5, 69, 70, 87, 88,
    148
  symbols, 70

C

Cancer, childhood (see Childhood
    cancer)
Caregivers, 2, 5, 30, 106, 123, 136,
    138, 139, 140, 142, 167

Cartoons, violence and death in, 20, 50, 96-97

Casket, 24, 68, 70, 75, 152, 153, 154, 155, 156, 159

Causality (*see* Subconcepts of death)

Cemetery, 56, 66, 87, 152, 155, 159
child's visits to, 156-157, 173
portrayal in artwork, 68, 70, 78, 79

Censorship, of music, 101-102

Center for Disease Control (CDC), 126

Cessation of bodily functions, 50, 60, 61, 73, 75 (*see also* Nonfunctionality)

Challenger Space Shuttle explosion, 25, 49

Chaplain (*see* Clergy)

Child
abuse of, 105, 146
anxiety concerning death, 23, 34, 35, 87, 135, 168
as a disadvantaged griever, 5, 163, 166, 168
death of, 18, 30, 31-32, 35, 37, 39, 56, 89, 131-132, 134, 140, 149, 150, 157, 158, 170
dying, 133, 135, 142, 143
feelings, 16, 25, 34, 40, 164-165, 166
impact of death on, 2, 16, 19, 26, 30, 148-149, 160, 164-165, 166, 167-168
of divorce, 126-128, 146
understanding of death, 10-13, 16, 20-24, 26, 29, 45-52, 56-70, 75, 77-82, 86-87, 95, 142, 151, 166, 170

Child bereavement (*see* Bereaved child)

Child development
cognitive, 1, 4, 10-11, 20-26, 56, 57-65, 68, 90, 97, 166
environmental influences on, 5, 22, 30, 33, 36, 48, 56, 103, 105, 110, 146, 150

[Child development]
gender differences in, 29-40, 109, 110, 113
motor, 57-58, 65
personality, 22, 45, 127
socialization, 3, 30, 33-36, 39-40, 51, 97, 100, 109-110, 145, 147
stages/phases of, 10-11, 20-26, 49, 50, 57-65, 75, 90
stereotyping, 21, 33, 37, 103, 109, 110

Childhood cancer/Child with cancer, 1, 5, 131-143
coping skills of family, 132-133, 135, 136, 138-139, 139-140, 141-142
cultural influences in
Japan, 140-141
China, 137-139
South Korea, 139-140
Taiwan, 134-136
cure, 131, 132, 133, 137, 138, 139, 142
death, 132, 133, 134, 135, 136, 140, 142, 143
hopes/wishes, 136, 138, 142, 143
incidence, 131-133
leukemia, 132, 135, 138
treatment, 132, 136, 138-139, 140, 141-142
tumors, 135, 136

Childhood Cancer Foundations, 135, 136, 137

China, management of childhood cancer in, 137-139

Chlamydia (*see* Sexuality)

Christianity, 88, 133, 134, 139, 146,

Chromosomes, gender differences in, 30

Church/Church attendance, 77, 124, 130, 139, 149, 154, 156

Classmate (*see* Peer; Student)

Clergy, 18, 24, 79, 87, 134, 142, 152, 153, 154, 155, 159, 174

Cognitive development
  adolescent, 22, 58-59, 64, 71-74,
    145
  child, 1, 4, 10-11, 20-26, 56,
    57-65, 68, 90, 97, 166
  models of, 26, 56, 57-58, 60
Colors, in artwork, 67, 75, 80, 86,
    87, 155
Commemoration of a death, 5, 25,
    158, 159, 174 (see also
    Memorialization)
Communication,
  concerning death, 3, 10, 12, 16,
    21, 25, 47, 49, 51, 52, 87, 142,
    157, 165, 167, 170
  guidelines for, 26, 51
  honesty in, 3, 9, 10, 25, 51, 90,
    129, 156, 170, 172
  open, 47, 48, 51, 52, 55, 154, 168,
    170
Concepts of death, 4, 10, 11, 12, 20,
    21, 29, 50, 56, 59, 60-65, 66,
    67, 68, 69, 71, 72-75, 89, 90,
    140 (see also Death; Subcon-
    cepts of death)
Conflict, 1, 64, 89, 96, 97, 98, 105,
    106, 109, 110, 140
Confusion of child concerning
    death, 2, 51, 90, 157, 165, 167,
    172
Coping with death, 16, 18, 24-26,
    29, 30, 34, 35, 55, 57, 133, 163,
    166, 168 (see also Adolescent;
    Bereaved child; Child;
    Childhood Cancer; Death)
Counter-culture, 100
Cremation, 70, 150
Cryogenics, 72
Culture/Cultural beliefs and
    influences, 1, 5, 34, 39, 64, 71,
    88, 95-96, 100, 124, 131,
    133-136, 137-141, 146
  African-American, 39, 104, 124
  Chinese, 137-139
  Egyptian, 149
  Hispanic, 124
  Japanese, 140-141

[Culture/Cultural beliefs and
    influences]
  Native American, 88, 124, 149,
    155
  Neanderthal, 149
  North American, 5, 17, 39, 61, 89,
    96, 98, 100, 109, 123, 126,
    129, 145, 146, 150, 151
  popular, 4, 71, 95, 103, 105
  South Korean, 139-140
  Taiwanese, 134-136
Cure, in childhood cancer, 131, 132,
    133, 137, 138, 139, 142

D

Death
  accidental, 19, 25, 37, 38, 39, 50,
    66, 68, 69, 73, 83, 84, 87, 89,
    100, 104, 132, 164, 165
  adolescent, 19, 35, 73
  AIDS, 127, 129, 157
  anniversary of a, 158, 159, 160
  anxiety concerning, 3, 9, 12, 23,
    29, 34, 35, 47, 55, 57, 74, 75,
    84, 87, 95, 168
  avoidance of, 3, 11, 21, 50, 51, 55,
    56, 67, 142, 150, 151, 172
  causes of, 19, 30, 33, 39, 69, 70,
    80, 81, 84
  child, 18, 30, 31-32, 35, 37, 39, 56,
    89, 131-132, 134, 140, 149,
    150, 157, 158, 170
  concepts/subconcepts of, 4, 10, 11,
    12, 20, 21, 29, 50, 56, 59,
    60-65, 66, 67, 68, 69, 71,
    72-75, 89, 90, 140
  education, 3, 10, 11, 17-18, 25,
    26, 46-49, 51, 55, 57, 158, 170,
    171
  family member, 16, 18, 19, 34, 49,
    56, 57, 69, 89, 127, 135, 147,
    149, 153, 170, 171, 174
  friend/peer, 18, 39, 56, 89, 150
  homicide/murder, 19, 36, 37, 38,
    39, 70, 80, 81, 87, 89, 100, 101,
    102, 104

[Death]
  incidence of, 20, 30, 32, 33, 38, 56, 73, 104, 134
  perceptions of, 1-5, 23, 55-90
  personification of, 67, 74, 75
  pet, 9, 11-12, 15, 18-19, 45, 51, 55
  reversibility of, 50, 58, 66, 75, 96-97
  rituals/rites, 1, 4, 5, 68, 69, 70, 75, 87, 88, 136, 147, 148, 152, 160, 163, 168
  secondary losses after, 167-168,
  sleep as, 10, 18, 21, 58, 66, 75, 86, 172
  sudden, 18, 24, 89, 171
  suicide, 2, 19, 35, 36, 37, 38, 39, 69, 73, 84, 89, 101, 102, 135
  understanding of, 10-13, 11, 16, 17, 18, 20-24, 26, 29, 45-52, 56-70, 64, 75, 77-82, 86-87, 90, 95, 142, 151, 159, 166, 170
Decision-making in the family, 133, 152, 154, 163
Delayed grief, 55, 152
Denial, 9, 13, 34, 72, 150
Devil, 79, 80, 87
Disadvantaged griever, child as a, 5, 163, 166, 168
Disasters, 25, 49, 50, 51, 69, 87, 104, 145
Divorce, 126-128, 146
Domestic violence, 2-3, 88, 104-105
Drawings (see Artwork)
Dreams, 2, 12, 34, 58, 73, 136, 169
Drug and alcohol abuse, 100, 102, 105, 124, 128

E

East Asia, 5, 131-143
Education
  AIDS, 123-126, 129-130
  childhood cancer, 133, 135, 137
  death, 3, 10, 11, 17-18, 25, 26, 46-49, 51, 55, 57, 158, 170, 171
Educators, role of, 1, 25, 30, 45-48, 58, 64, 106, 133, 158

Egocentricity/Ego development, 24, 57, 58
Elderly (see Old age)
Emotional pain (see Pain)
Emotions (see feelings under Adolescence/Adolescent; Adult; Child; War)
Empathy, 52, 96, 123
Ethical issues concerning life and death, 50, 63, 72, 90
Ethnicity (see Culture/Cultural beliefs and influences)
Euthanasia, 90, 135

F

Family/Family member
  bereaved, 16, 24, 25, 50, 56, 147, 149, 150, 151, 152-160
  characteristics of, 34, 56-57, 88, 95, 110, 123, 124, 145, 146, 149-151
  childhood cancer, 132-143
  extended, 56-57, 134, 136, 139, 149, 150,
  instability of, 102, 105
  nuclear, 56, 134, 145, 149, 150
  roles within, 34, 72, 95, 145, 146, 147, 149
  separation of, 57, 72, 126, 140, 145, 146
Fantasy, use of, 11, 17, 49, 50, 58, 66, 86 (see also Imagination)
Fears (see also Anxiety)
  abandonment, 58
  death, 3, 9, 12, 23, 29, 34, 35, 47, 55, 57, 74, 75, 84, 87, 95, 168
  mutilation, 50, 68, 75, 96, 99
  separation, 50, 58, 66, 68, 75
  suffocation, 69, 75
Finality of death (see Irreversibility)
Friend, death of, 3, 55, 73, 74, 89
Fortune teller, role of, 134, 136
Funeral, 145-159, 163-174
  attendance at/participation in, 24, 74, 95, 129, 150, 151, 156, 159, 163, 168-169, 172, 173, 174

[Funeral]
avoidance of, 150-151, 173, 174
director's role in, 150, 152, 156, 159
home, 56, 154, 156
preparation for, 16, 169, 173
rituals/rites, 4, 5, 26, 69, 70, 75, 87, 88, 145-150, 152-160, 164
role of, 5, 20, 80, 81, 87, 152, 160, 164-165
services, 5, 49, 148, 149, 150, 153, 154, 156, 159
wake, 49

G

Games, 4, 24, 45, 142 (see also Toys)
socialization role of, 36-37, 100
Gender/Gender differences, 1, 3, 5, 61, 89 (see also Adolescence; Aggression; Artwork; Child development; Play; Suicide; Violence; and War)
attitudes/feelings toward war, 89, 109, 113
incidence of death, 29-33, 38
research on, 5, 29-30, 34-36, 89, 103, 109, 110, 115-116
socialization, 3, 30, 33-35, 39, 40, 103, 109
stereotyping, 21, 33, 37, 103, 109-110
understanding of death, 29-40
Genetic research, 30, 33, 40, 72, 90
God, 25, 77, 78, 80, 81, 82, 86, 87, 101, 154, 172
Grandchildren, 16, 149, 150, 159, 173-174
Grandparent,
death of, 9, 11, 12, 18, 19, 69, 147, 153, 149, 150, 153, 156, 158, 160, 171, 174
role of, 15-16, 56-57, 95, 136, 141, 142, 171, 173
Grief/Grieving, 12, 13, 20, 29, 45, 96, 127, 152, 154

[Grief/Grieving]
child, 2, 3, 5, 11, 55, 89, 157, 163, 165, 166-168, 171
family member, 9, 25, 157, 164, 169, 171, 173
tasks of, 5, 26, 55, 147, 151, 152-155, 157, 166
Group, support (see Bereavement support group; Support)
Guilt, 167
Gulf War (see War)
Guns, 36, 37, 100, 104, 112, 113
control of, 39-40

H

Health care, 106, 132-133, 134, 136, 138, 139, 140, 142-143
Heaven, 25, 69, 78-79, 81-82, 84, 86-87, 170, 172
Hell, 69, 81-82, 87, 101
Helplessness, 140, 169
HIV (see AIDS)
Homicide (see Death)
Homosexuality, 123, 128-129
Honesty (see Communication)
Hope, 2, 112, 113, 136, 137, 138, 139, 143
Hospice care, 2, 133, 136, 138, 140, 143
Hospital/Hospitalization, 2, 11, 46, 56, 66, 123, 134, 135, 137, 138, 139, 140, 141, 142, 150, 164, 170, 171, 173-174

I

Illness (see Life-threatening illness)
Imagination (see also Fantasy), 24, 50, 55, 66, 73, 153, 163
Immortality of youth, 72, 150-151 (see also Adolescence/ Adolescent)
Independence, 34, 68, 71-72, 145-146, 147, 151 (see also Adolescence/Adolescent)

Inevitability of death (*see* universality under Subconcepts of death)

Infant deaths, 18, 30, 56, 157

Invulnerability (*see* Adolescence/ Adolescent)

Irreversibility (*see also* Subconcepts of death)
in medical technology, 63-64, 67, 69, 72, 73, 90

J

Japan/Japanese Culture, 102, 131, 132, 133, 134, 139, 140-143

L

Leavetaking, 164

Letter writing as grief work (*see* Narrative; Story/Storytelling)

Leukemia (*see* Childhood Cancer)

Life, 2, 3, 4, 9, 11, 16, 21, 25, 60, 105
after death, 69, 72, 74, 84, 86, 87, 148
cycle, 13, 19, 26, 63, 67, 69, 71, 149, 150, 160, 164, 166
expectancy, 20, 30, 31, 40
experiences, 1, 22, 23, 24, 45-52, 56-57
support measures, 64, 72, 73, 90
symbols in artwork, 68, 70, 75, 82, 86
value of, 4, 18, 40, 95, 90

Life-threatening illness, 2, 88, 131-143, 163 (*see also* Childhood cancer)

Loneliness, 74

Losses, 2, 26, 167-168 (*see also* Death; Secondary losses)

Love, 12, 13, 86, 100, 101, 112, 163, 165, 168, 171, 174, 176

M

Magical thinking in childhood (*see* Fantasy; Imagination)

Male (*see* Gender/Gender differences)

Mature understanding of death, 1, 4, 56, 60, 62, 63, 64, 89

Media
advertising, 98, 100, 106
AIDS in, 123, 124, 128-129
portrayal of death by, 20, 52, 57, 96-97, 150
role of, 1, 98, 103, 106
violence in, 1, 4-5, 36, 39, 40, 50, 89, 90, 96, 97, 99, 104
vulnerability of child/adolescent to, 98, 127

Medical technology, 64, 72, 73, 90

Memorialization, 158-165 (*see also* Commemoration)

Minnesota Multi-phasic Personality Inventory (MMPI), 127-128

Morality, 22, 87, 110, 141

Mortality (*see* Death)

Mourning (*see* Grief/Grieving)

Murder (*see* homicide under Death)

Music, 100-103
drug and alcohol abuse in, 100, 102
socialization role, 36, 101-103
suicide in, 36, 101, 102
violence in, 4, 36, 101-103

Mutilation
anxiety, 68, 75
body, 50, 68, 96, 99

N

Narrative, 158 (*see also* Story/ Storytelling)

Native American traditions and practices, 88, 124, 149, 155

Neanderthal traditions and practices, 148-149

News (*see* Media)

Nightmares (*see* Dreams)

Nonfunctionality (*see* Cessation of bodily functions; Subconcepts of death)

Nuclear family, 56, 134, 145, 149, 150

Nurse/Nursing practice, 135, 138, 150, 158
Nurturing, 52, 166

O

Old age/Older generation (*see also* Grandparent), 29, 30, 50, 66, 67, 69, 75, 81, 83, 95, 102, 134, 139
Oncology/Oncologist (*see* Pediatric Oncology)
Open communication (*see* Communication)
Organ transplants, 69, 72, 90, 139

P

Pain
  emotional, 11, 13, 51, 55, 68, 96, 140, 165, 166, 169, 171
  physical, 25, 70, 131, 135, 136, 138-139, 140, 141
Palliative care, 2, 136, 138
Parent
  death education role, 3, 10, 11, 17-18, 25, 26, 46-49, 51, 55, 57, 170, 171
  dying, 22, 56, 89, 149, 166
  protective role, 3, 9, 18, 52, 55, 142, 150, 151, 163, 168, 169, 171
  support group, 132, 137, 142
Pediatric hospice (*see* Hospice Care)
Pediatric oncology/oncologist, 135, 138
Peer (*see also* Friend; Student)
  death of, 18, 56, 89, 150
  relationships, 23, 37, 71-72, 99, 103, 165, 166
People's Republic of China (PRC) (*see* China)
Persian Gulf War (*see* War)
Personality development (*see* Child development)
Personification of death, 67, 74, 75
Pet
  death of, 9, 11-12, 15, 18-19, 45, 51, 55

[Pet]
  role/value of, 2, 11-12, 19
Physical pain (*see* Pain)
Physician, role of, 66, 135, 138, 142
Pictures (*see also* Artwork)
  sharing of, 158, 159
Play,
  aggression/violence in, 37, 100
  games/toys used in, 100
  gender differences in, 33, 37
  portrayal of death in, 16, 24
  role of, 2, 3, 16, 24, 137, 138, 174
Political conflict (*see* War)
Popular culture, 4, 95-106
Pregnancy, 15, 125, 128
Problem-solving ability, 58, 59, 68
Professionals
  death education role, 1, 5, 9, 10, 45, 55, 57, 64, 90, 95, 123, 163, 166
  health care role, 2, 20, 142-143
Protection of child, 3, 9, 18, 52, 55, 142, 150, 151, 163, 168, 169, 171

Q

Quality of life in childhood cancer, 132, 133, 138

R

Rabbi (*see* Clergy)
Rap music, 36, 100, 101-102
Reasoning (*see* Cognitive development)
Rebellion (*see* Adolescence/Adolescent)
Reconciliation of grief, 152
Religion/Religious beliefs and traditions
  Buddhism, 133, 134, 141
  Christian, 88, 95, 133, 134, 139, 146
  Confucian, 133-134, 137, 141
  folk, 134
  Judaism, 146

[Religion/Religious beliefs and traditions]
  Protestant, 76
  Roman Catholic, 76
  Shammanist, 134
  Shinto, 133, 141
Repression of feelings, 34
Republic of China (ROC) (*see* Taiwan)
Research study
  aggression/violence, 5, 34-35, 97, 102, 109-121
  AIDS, 124, 128
  artwork, 65-70, 74, 77-86
  childhood bereavement, 127
  childhood cancer, 131-143
  divorce, 126-128, 146
  gender differences, 5, 29-30, 34-36, 89, 103, 109, 110, 115-116
  genetics, 30, 33, 40, 72, 90
  media/music/television/toys, 97, 99, 100, 101, 102, 103, 104
  suicide, 35-37, 39
  understanding of death, 4, 21, 22, 23, 29, 57, 58, 59-61, 64, 67, 74, 75, 76, 88, 89
  war, 109-121
Reversibility of death (*see* Death)
Risk-taking behavior (*see* Adolescence/Adolescent)
Rituals/Rites, 145-160
  Asian culture, 131-143
  burial, 4, 5, 69-70, 87, 88, 148
  child participation in, 145-160, 163-176
  death, 1, 4, 5, 68, 69, 70, 75, 87, 88, 136, 147, 148, 152, 160, 163, 168
  funeral, 4, 5, 26, 69, 70, 75, 87, 88, 145-150, 152-160, 164
  remembrance, 141
Rock music/lyrics, 36, 100-101, 102
Role model, 71, 105, 106, 164
Rural society (see Society)

S

Sadness, 12, 16, 17, 25, 69, 70, 74, 79, 84, 87, 112, 113, 140, 151, 167, 168, 174, 176
Satanic practices, 36, 99, 101
School
  aggression/violence, 40, 104, 105
  bereaved child, 34, 165, 166, 170
  death of staff member/student, 19, 158
  intervention program, 40, 46
  research study, 109-121
  role of, 3, 52, 95, 106, 129, 130
Secondary losses after death, 167-168
Self-image, 23, 50, 151
Sensationalism of violence, 4-5, 89
Separation anxiety, 50, 58, 66, 68, 75
Sex differences (*see* Gender/Gender differences)
Sexuality/Sexual Activity
  adolescent, 71-72, 124, 125-126
  AIDS epidemic, 123-130
  AIDS (HIV) survey, 46, 124-127, 128
Sexually Transmitted Diseases (STD) 125-127, 128
Sibling
  bereaved, 13, 153, 159, 170, 171
  death, 19, 49, 56, 89, 149, 170
  of child with cancer, 132, 135, 136, 140
Social support (*see* Support)
Social worker, role of, 163
Socialization
  child (*see* Child development)
  games/toys, 36-37, 100
  gender differences, 3, 30, 33-35, 39, 40, 103, 109
  media/television/music, 36, 97, 99, 101-104
Society/Societal Expectations and Influences, 1, 3, 5, 17, 19, 30, 33, 34, 39, 40, 57, 59, 71, 90, 95, 99, 102, 103, 109, 124, 145, 147, 148, 160

[Society/Societal Expectations and Influences]
death attitude system, 20, 55
rural, 56, 133, 134, 137, 142, 170
urban, 56, 124, 133, 134, 150
Sorrow (see Sadness)
Soul/Spirit, 74, 81, 82, 83, 86, 87, 141, 148
South Korea/South Korean Culture, 132, 133, 134, 139-140, 141, 142
Spirituality, 2, 24 (see also Religion/Religious beliefs and traditions)
Stage/phase of child development (see Adolescence/Adolescent; Child development)
Stereotyping (see Gender/Gender differences)
Story/Storytelling, 1, 2, 15-16, 115, 165, 166 (see also Narrative)
Student, 3, 5, 15, 17, 34, 36, 46, 62, 64, 104, 110-111, 113, 124-129, 158
Subconcepts of death (see also Concepts of death; Death)
causality, 4, 61, 62, 64, 66, 67, 69, 72, 73, 75, 89
irreversibility, 10, 11, 21, 50, 59, 60-64, 66, 67, 68, 72, 73, 74, 75, 89, 90,
nonfunctionality, 4, 50, 60-64, 66, 67, 69, 72, 73, 74, 75, 89
universality, 4, 11, 12, 21, 50, 59, 60-64, 66, 67, 68, 71, 72, 74, 75, 89, 90, 140
Substance abuse (see Drug and alcohol abuse)
Sudden death (see Death)
Suffering, 2, 55, 69, 70, 96, 131, 146, 169, 171
of surrogate, 152
Suffocation anxiety, 69, 75
Suicide (see also Adolescence/Adolescent; Death)
gender differences in, 35, 39
incidence, 19, 37, 73,

[Suicide]
research on, 35-37, 39
role of media/music in promoting, 36, 89, 101, 102
Support
child/adolescent bereavement group, 3, 26, 164, 167, 170, 171
emotional, 135, 136, 138, 140, 160, 165, 166
life, 64, 73
parent group, 135, 137, 142
peer, 37, 72, 165, 166
social, 2, 34, 40, 52, 73, 127, 135, 136, 147, 151, 154, 155, 159, 164, 165
Symbolism, use of, 50, 57, 65, 68, 70, 75, 82, 86, 87, 133
Sympathy, 12, 35

T

Taboo, death as a, 29, 57, 159 (see also Avoidance of death; Banishment of death)
Taiwan, 131, 132, 133, 134-136, 137, 142
Tasks of grieving (mourning) (see Grief/Grieving)
Teachable moments, 4, 25, 46-48, 51-52
Teacher, role of, 127, 128, 136
Team (see Health care)
Teen bereavement support group (see Support)
Teenager (see Adolescence)
Television, 96-99 (see also Media)
advertising, 98, 100, 106
gender stereotyping, 103
portrayal of death, 9, 48 49, 96
regulation of, 97-98, 105, 106
socialization role, 36, 89, 99, 102
violence on, 36, 96-97, 98, 99, 104
Terminal care (see Palliative care)

Toys, 4, 36, 37, 45, 100, 142 (*see also* Games)
Tribute, 159, 174 (*see also* Rituals/rites)
Trust, 11, 48
Truthtelling (*see* Communication; Honesty)

U

Understanding of death (*see* Adolescence/Adolescent; Adult; Child; and Death)
United Nations, 131
United States, 18, 19, 36, 39, 50, 56, 61, 97, 98, 125, 132, 134, 135, 142, 143, 146, 149
Universality (*see* Subconcepts of death)
Unknown, fear of, 9, 25, 168
Urban society (*see* Society)

V

VCR, 98, 99
Venereal disease (*see* Sexually Transmitted Diseases)
Victims, 96
  disaster, 51-52
  violence, 40, 97, 103, 104
  war, 140
Viet Nam War, 115
Violence/Violent Acts, 1, 3, 88, 98 (*see also* Aggression; War)
  adolescent, 35, 36, 39, 104, 110
  at home and in the community, 3, 88, 104-105
  death from, 40, 51, 66, 87
  games/toys, 24, 37, 100
  gender differences, 35, 37, 103, 109, 110, 112, 113, 114, 115, 118-121

[Violence/Violent Acts]
  media's portrayal of, 1, 4-5, 36, 39, 40, 50, 89, 90, 96, 97, 99, 104
  music's portrayal of, 4, 36, 100-102, 103
  popular culture, 4, 95-106
  racial differences, 39, 104
  tolerance of, 5, 114
Visitation (*see* Funeral)
Vulnerability, 4, 25, 100

W

Wake, 49
War, 20, 51, 64, 69, 83, 89, 104
  artwork, 110, 112, 113, 115, 118-121
  attitudes/feelings, 89, 109, 113, 115
  gender differences, 37, 109, 110, 113, 114, 115, 118-121
  grade/age differences, 110, 113, 115
  Persian Gulf War, 5, 109-121
  toys, 37, 100
Weapons, 36, 37, 39, 40, 100, 104, 105, 112, 113, 114
Will-making, 46
Wishes (*see* Childhood Cancer; Hope)
Withdrawal, 147
World Health Organization (WHO), 138
Writings (*see* Narrative; Story/Storytelling)

Y

Youth (*see* Adolescence)